Brainfit

*10 Minutes a Day
for a Sharper Mind and Memory*

CORINNE L. GEDIMAN
WITH FRANCIS M. CRINELLA, Ph.D.

RUTLEDGE HILL PRESS

Nashville, Tennessee
A Division of Thomas Nelson Publishers
www.ThomasNelson.com

Published by Rutledge Hill Press, a Division of Thomas Nelson, Inc., P.O. Box 141000, Nashville, Tennessee, 37214.

Rutledge Hill Press books may be purchased in bulk for educational, business, fundraising, or sales promotional use. For information, please e-mail SpecialMarkets@ThomasNelson.com.

Library of Congress Cataloging-in-Publication Data

Gediman, Corinne, 1949-
  Brainfit : 10 minutes a day for a sharper mind and memory / Corinne Gediman.
    p. cm.
Includes bibliographical references.
    ISBN 1-4016-0223-1 (pbk.)
    1. Mnemonics. 2. Intellect. I. Title.
    BF385.G43 2005
    153.1'4—dc22

                                        20050195101-4016-0223-1

Printed in the United States of America

05 06 07 08 09—9 8 7 6 5 4 3 2 1

To my parents Harry and Laura Lille,
who taught me that life is a precious gift
and learning is the window that opens us up
to a rich and beautiful world full of possibilities.

Contents

Acknowledgments

I'd like to say a special thank-you to the following people who helped make this book possible:

- Pamela Clements, Geoff Stone, and the entire supportive staff at Rutledge Hill Press for making *Brainfit* a reality
- Coleen O'Shea, my literary agent, for her wisdom and guidance
- Dr. Francis Crinella, my "guardian angel," for his mentorship and intellectual contributions
- Anne Louise Gittleman, the First Lady of Nutrition, for opening the window
- Bonnie Lynn Simon, Ph.D., for her design input and moral support
- Julie Paige for her creative input and keeping me on task
- Barbara Bushner for her expertise in the self-help book market
- Barry Gediman for always believing in me

Foreword

Some individuals seem to have a better memory than others, and there is a wide belief that a strong memory capacity is a God-given talent that has been bestowed on some but not all. We often hear people complain about their poor or worsening memory and are sympathetic but at the same time chalk it up to the inevitable. It may even be you who has a poorer memory capacity than others and has come to accept the cultural stereotype that the gap between your present day memory capacity and that of your youth will only widen. Is there nothing that can be done to improve memory, or is memory capacity an immutable hereditary trait like red hair or blue eyes?

In 1985, at the University of California, Irvine, we began a major research experiment to find out if age-related decline in memory was an inevitable consequence of aging or whether something might be done to reverse the process—or at least slow it down. Several hundred retired, senior citizens took part in a program of daily activities that were designed to improve physical and mental health, including mental exercises that were thought to be useful in slowing down age-related memory decline. To our delight, when we re-tested our senior citizens in 1990, we found that a program of daily mental exercises did put the brakes on age-related decline in mental functions, including memory. In some cases, seventy-five year olds were better at playing a wide number of mental games than they had been five years earlier. Standardized tests of memory showed a slowing of the rate of mental decline in some and actual improvement in others. This was one of the earliest experiments to demonstrate that memory decline was not an inevitable by-product of aging. How might this dramatic improvement have occurred? We now know that even among senior citizens a process called "neural plasticity" is present-the brain continues to change or remodel itself in order to improve mental functioning, even in eighty and ninety year olds!

Memory is the best evidence for the presence of neural plasticity. An older person, after reading the morning paper, knows something now that he or she did not know before. Depending on how important the new information might be, and how well it becomes organized in the person's memory banks, the information will remain available for recall and use. Neural plasticity is also evident when we fail to remember information that was once known-forgetting. Erasing what was once important but now less important, or what was once believed to be true but is now known to be false, leads to a less cluttered and more efficient mind.

When we started the senior citizen's research program, we did not have a formal mental training program. We believed that mental activity could improve memory but had to craft our own set of mental exercises on a trial and error basis—nothing like Brainfit was available. Now, in the following pages, the reader will find a systematic set of exercises, each adapted from the latest research on human memory, which have been carefully designed and sequenced so that memory and mental efficiency will improve. Each exercise has been designed to challenge the student, and the format is such that each challenge will be enjoyable. The outcome of the Brainfit program will, of course, depend on the commitment and diligence of the student, but there is no doubt that with a modest effort, memory and mental efficiency are bound to improve.

Francis M. Crinella, Ph.D.
Clinical Professor of Pediatrics,
Psychiatry & Human Behavior, and
Physical Medicine & Rehabilitation
University of California, Irvine

Chapter One

Regain Your Brain

*"The mind is like a parachute . . .
it doesn't work unless it is open."*
—ANONYMOUS

A Modern Fairy Tale

Imagine a now middle-aged Sleeping Beauty and Prince Charming. They've had a little cosmetic surgery, work out regularly at the health club, eat a low-carb diet and attend Pilates classes regularly. They check their good and bad cholesterol yearly, drink a glass of red wine a day, and indulge in the occasional massage. Aging well is a top priority, and they understand the importance of a healthy lifestyle.

Every morning, they ask the magic mirror the proverbial question (with a twenty-first century twist). "Mirror, mirror on the wall, who is the youngest of us all?" The mirror answers back, "You guys look awesome, but may I suggest a PET brain scan to check out your aging brain? After all, what good is an attractive and fit body if you are not going to be mentally present to enjoy it?!"

And the moral of the story is . . . "Don't forget to make brain fitness part of your antiaging strategy."

Searching for the Fountain of Youth

Henry Wadsworth Longfellow once said, "Youth comes but once in a lifetime." If Mr. Longfellow were alive today, he would marvel at how the scientific advances of the twenty-first century are creating ways for us to rejuvenate ourselves and live well into our nineties. Science and medicine are allowing us to replace aging body parts, transplant thinning hair, revitalize our libido, as well as nip, tuck, and lift anything that sags. But staying young is not just a matter of physical fitness and cardiovascular health; it is also a matter of brain fitness. For those who seek the fountain of youth, it's time to make brain fitness the next battleground on the antiaging front. Before you don your brain gladiator attire, however, it's helpful to understand what you have working for you and against you. So, let's begin with an understanding of how the brain ages.

Unraveling the Mystery of Brain Aging

In recent years, we have explored the surface of Mars, mapped the human genome, and cloned sheep. By contrast scientists are only just beginning to understand the processes associated with brain aging. Numerous factors, however, are colliding and catapulting neuroscience (the study of the brain and nervous system) to the forefront of medical research. First, people are living longer, giving us more aging brains to study and protect. The average life span today is seventy-five years, up forty-seven years from 1900. Scientists predict that life expectancy by the middle of the twenty-first century could be well into the nineties and beyond. Running parallel to increased life span is new brain imaging technology such as MRI (magnetic resonance imaging) and PET (positron emission tomography), which allows scientists to explore the surfaces of the aging brain and detect miniscule changes in brain anatomy. Finally, we have the baby boomers, seventy-nine million individuals strong, who are rapidly increasing the ranks of senior citizens, turning fifty at the rate of ten thousand per day; and they do not intend to age silently. Always a vocal group, the baby boomers are demanding to know what can be done to preserve their bodies and their brains.

What we are learning about the aging brain is dispelling old myths and opening up new avenues of research and treatment. Until very recently, brain aging was attributed to the ongoing loss of brain cells (neurons) through a natural biological process called apoptosis. According to Will Block, publisher and editorial director of *Life Enhancement* magazine, " of the roughly 100 billion neurons in the brain, we lose . . . permanently . . . about 100,000 daily."[1] Only a decade ago, the prevailing theory of brain aging was based on the premise that an irrevocable loss of brain cells throughout our lifetime would result in progressive mental decline and eventual senility. Scientists now know this is not true. In fact, it is not the number of brain cells you have but the health of existing brain cells that determines brain resilience.

More recent studies suggest that the plaques and tangles that begin accumulating in the brain by our late twenties may be the critical factor in brain aging. Dr. Gary Small describes this phenomenon in his book *The Memory Bible*.[2] He explains that "the subtle, gradual aging of the brain starts as tiny plaques and tangles that begin accumulating there, decades before a doctor can recognize any symptoms. . . . In fact, these plaques and tangles begin forming so early in our adult lives that subtle memory and language changes go unnoticed and ignored for many years."

While the accumulation of plaques and tangles is an acknowledged factor in brain aging, new research studies suggest that this buildup of plaques and tangles may be just the tip of the iceberg when it comes to understanding and reversing brain aging. A recent *USC Health* magazine article entitled "The Aging Brain" cites new research suggesting that the root cause of brain aging may reside in complex chemical interactions that occur in the brain over time, as well as inflammatory processes associated with aging.[3]

While the many different theories of brain aging compete for attention and funding, there are two points on which all scientists seem to agree: cognitive decline is not due to normal brain cell loss, and the mystery of brain aging will take generations of scientists to unravel.

The Amazing Brain

One of the most amazing findings arising from recent brain research is confirmation that the brain is a dynamic organ that continually rewires and adapts itself, even in old age. The miraculous regenerative powers of the brain are being seen in both the formation of new brain cells and the expansion of new neural connections between brain cells. Princeton University researcher Elizabeth Gould, studying macaque monkeys, reported in 1999 that the mature primate brain produces new neurons that incorporate themselves into the neocortex—the thinking center of the brain.[4] In a January 2002 review in the journal *Nature Neuroscience*, Pasko Rakic and David Kornack reported spotting new brain cells in the hippocampus region of the brain, which is associated with learning and memory.[5]

Perhaps most hopeful is data indicating that lifestyle choices, which are under our control, can hasten or slow down brain aging. Of particular interest are studies confirming that challenging the brain early and often builds cognitive reserve and boosts the brain's own regenerative processes. In his book *Mozart's Brain and the Fighter Pilot,* Dr. Richard Restak explains the effect of mental stimulation on brain health this way: "throughout our lives the brain retains a high degree of plasticity; it changes in response to experience. If the experiences are rich and varied, the brain will develop a greater number of nerve cell connections. If the experiences are dull and infrequent, the connections will either never form or die off."[6] By regularly exercising our brain's mental functions we can build a stronger and healthier brain.

Memory Changes with Age

Since most of us do not have access to expensive brain scanning equipment, we must rely on more subjective measures of our own brain aging. One of the first and earliest signs of brain aging in healthy adults is a change in memory. In fact, memory peaks in our late twenties. So if you are experiencing the occasional memory cramp, you are not alone. A recent study by Bruskin/Goldring Research questions doctors about memory loss issues with their patients. More than 80 percent of all physicians surveyed said their patients over age thirty complained of memory loss. Another study by the Dana Foundation revealed that nearly seven of ten adults have concerns about memory decline.[7]

Knowing you have plenty of company is not necessarily comforting. With the threat of Alzheimer's disease looming, most people want to know whether their memory failures fall within the normal range. Unless you are in the minority of people suffering from a real disease of the brain, the memory changes you are experiencing are perfectly normal. As reported in a *Newsweek* issue on memory, Dr. Fergus Craik of the Rotman Research Institute explains normal memory changes this way: "Memory processes are not lost to us as we age. . . . The mechanism is not broken, it's just inefficient."[8] The inefficiencies we notice as we age usually involve recent memories rather than distant, past ones, according to Dr. Gary Small.[9]

Still, it is helpful to have general guidelines by which to assess what's normal and what's not. Below is a checklist that shows the range of memory loss from benign to severe in middle-aged and older people. A more detailed checklist developed by the Memory Research Department of the University of Wisconsin can be found at *www .medicine.wise.edu/mainweb/DOMPages.php?section=DOM&page=main*. Additionally, The Alzheimer's Foundation of America provides, free of charge, a wealth of information about memory loss and treatment.[10]

Early, Usually Benign, Signs of Memory Loss
- Occasionally having trouble finding the right word
- Momentarily "blanking" on the name of a familiar acquaintance or colleague
- Temporarily misplacing your keys or wallet
- Momentarily forgetting what day of the week it is
- Forgetting once or twice to turn off the stove
- Forgetting an item on your To Do list
- Forgetting an occasional meeting or appointment
- Getting disoriented in a giant mall
- Not recognizing someone you met a long time ago

Signs of Severe Memory Loss
- Difficulty naming common objects
- Difficulty in understanding words
- Substituting inappropriate words, making sentences unintelligible
- Asking the same questions over and over again
- Putting common objects in inappropriate places, like putting an iron in the freezer and not recalling how it got there
- Not knowing the date, time, or year
- Wearing clothes inappropriately, like a winter jacket on a hot summer day
- Forgetting important appointments repeatedly
- Getting lost on one's own street
- Not knowing where you are or how you got there

Other Changes Associated with Severe Memory Loss
- Rapid mood swings and irritability for no apparent reason
- Extreme personality changes, like changing from a person who is generally easy and open to one who is suspicious and fearful
- Inability to perform common household chores, like setting a table

- Inability to perform tasks involving simple calculations, like balancing a checkbook
- Noticeable and inexplicable confusion at home or in the workplace

Fitness from the Neck Up

If you are reading this book, there is an excellent chance that reviewing the memory checklist brought you a sense of relief . . . "I'm okay after all." Still, scientists agree it is easier to preserve memory and mental agility than it is to try and regain it. Think of it this way: would you wait until you couldn't lift your briefcase into the overhead compartment of the plane to start a muscle mass rebuilding program? Of course not—so why wait until your brain cells atrophy to start exercising your brain? The brain can't exercise itself. It needs your help. Choosing to have a healthier brain is a personal lifestyle choice. While most people understand the correlation between physical fitness and a longer, healthier life, few people extend the analogy to include fitness from the neck up. Most people would agree, however, that quality of life as we age is absolutely dependent on healthy brain functioning. What good is a long life if our mental capacities are going soft?

Scientists and medical professionals are sounding the brain health alarm. The Alzheimer's Association has a national radio spot that advocates, "Stay active, eat healthy, and make brain health a personal and national priority." The message is clear. It's time to take exercising our brain as seriously as we take physical exercise and dietary health. We can actively influence the health of our brains by engaging in a planned program of brain aerobics. The choice is ours. We can sit back and hope that genetics play in our favor, or we can take an active role in building and protecting our brains, starting today.

What Are the Best Brain Fitness Exercises?

The brain thrives on novelty, so the best brain fitness exercises are those that make us think in new ways and are enjoyable. No matter how good an exercise is if it becomes boring and routine we are unlikely to follow through on a regular basis. How many of us have exercise equipment gathering dust in the basement or a spare bedroom? The mental exercises and hobbies in which you choose to engage must be stimulating and fun if you are going to practice them on a regular basis. Good brain fitness exercises include the following criteria:

1. Force you to think while doing them
   - assembling a model airplane
   - answering questions on television quiz shows
   - creating a new recipe from scratch
   - doing crossword puzzles or brainteasers

2. Challenge you to do old things in new ways
   - taking a new route home from work
   - brushing your teeth with your nondominant hand
   - eating your dinner with chopsticks

3. Include progressive levels of new learning
   - learning a new language
   - taking up a new hobby
   - learning how to use a new software application
   - learning or relearning how to play a musical instrument

4. Require new modes of thinking
   - writing a rhyming poem
   - building a sand castle or ice sculpture
   - drawing a picture
   - writing your memoirs
   - reading a new book genre (e.g., biography instead of fiction)

5. Involve body-kinesthetic challenge
   - cross-country skiing, golf, tennis, Ping-Pong, or pool
   - learning how to drive a standard shift automobile
   - riding a bicycle
   - creating art through painting, pottery, or woodworking
   - ballroom dancing

6. Are socially interactive
   - playing bridge or other card games
   - participating in book club discussions
   - doing volunteer work

- taking classes at a community college
- attending a play or a lecture with friends

7. Aerobic exercises, which pump blood and important nutrients to the brain
   - walking briskly or jogging
   - walking or running on a treadmill
   - working out on an elliptical cross-trainer
   - taking "spin" classes or step aerobics classes
   - doing jumping jacks

How Does the *Brainfit* Program Work?

The *Brainfit* program is a guided brain exercise program designed to put you on the fast track to fitness from the neck up. It is modeled on circuit training, one of the hottest trends in physical fitness training. In circuit training, exercisers move rapidly from one fitness station to another, spending five or ten minutes at each station. Fitness stations alternate between cardiovascular workouts and muscle building workouts. The huge popularity of circuit training is attributed to people's desire for a total exercise regimen which is also fast, fun, and effective.

Building on the gains and enjoyment people experience in circuit training, the *Brainfit* program consists of nine brain-boosting workout stations. Each station focuses on strengthening a different aspect of memory and mental agility. Daily exercises, which take approximately ten minutes to complete, are high impact and fun. The nine fitness stations with their primary exercise focus are described below:

Fitness Station	Exercise Focus
Making Memories	Exercises for short-term and long-term memory
Taking Aim	Exercises using the fundamental memory skills
Remembering Who	Exercises for remembering names
Remembering What	Exercises for remembering that To Do list
Remembering How Many	Exercises for remembering important numbers
Remembering When	Exercises for remembering appointments and special occasions

Fitness Station	Exercise Focus
Remembering Where	Exercises for remembering directions and locating misplaced objects
Mental Agility—Left Brain	Exercises for verbal challenge
Mental Agility—Right Brain	Exercises for visual-spatial challenges

The *Brainfit* program works like a personal trainer guiding you through the exercises, providing feedback, and helping you to assess your personal gains. Special features of the *Brainfit* program include daily workouts, memory and mental agility assessments, lifestyle health tips, and a lifestyle action planner.

Tips for a Successful Workout

It is normal to approach brain fitness training with a little anxiety. After all, you are embarking on a new challenge. So here are some tips that will help make your *Brainfit* workout experience both productive and fun.

1. Relax and have fun. Brain fitness is not a test and there are no scores. Did you know that worry and stress actually interfere with the brain's mental processes?
2. By learning and following the *Brainfit* program, you are challenging your brain. When your brain is challenged, your brain cells begin firing messages between existing neurons, which in turn strengthens neural connections. In other words, simply by participating in the *Brainfit* program, your brain is getting stronger and you are getting smarter. You're a winner no matter what!
3. Don't expect a perfect memory. Human beings forget occasionally. Would you really want to remember every fleeting piece of information you encounter? Better to actively choose to remember the important things, and let the rest go.
4. Focus on what you *can* remember, not on what you can't remember. Don't be too hard on yourself. Instead, feel good about your mental accomplishments.
5. The exercises in the *Brainfit* program are "hands-on" and interactive, so have a pencil or pen handy.
6. To achieve maximum gains, follow the established progression of the fitness stations and participate in all of the weekly exercises.

7. Pace yourself. It is best to focus on one fitness station per week. This will give you an opportunity to practice new skills and secure your brain fitness gains before proceeding to the next fitness station.

8. Practice and transfer your new memory and mental agility skills regularly in your everyday life. Achieving measurable gains requires dedication and commitment.

9. Remember there is no magic pill. Brain fitness and memory enhancement are part of an ongoing antiaging strategy that promises you and your loved ones a better quality of life.

10. Celebrate your successes.

Creating a Baseline

Before embarking on a fitness program, it's helpful to have a baseline assessment of your strengths and areas for improvement. Baseline assessments are helpful in two ways: they provide a way to measure gains and help pinpoint the memory and mental agility areas needing the most attention during your workout. When it comes to assessing memory, medical professionals typically rely on both subjective and objective memory assessments. With mental agility assessments, objective assessments are usually preferred. Subjective assessments can be self-administered while objective assessments are usually administered and scored by a second party. For our purposes, you will score all of your own assessments.

The *Brainfit* program incorporates both pre-assessments and post-assessments. The following three pre-assessments will help you rate your current memory and mental agility fitness. In Chapter Eleven you will be invited to take three post-assessments to rate improvements in your memory and mental agility fitness.

Subjective Memory Pre-Assessment [11]

Subjective assessments are based on our own perceptions of how well we think we are doing with regard to specific memory functions. Most people are aware of changes in their memory over time and are able to respond to subjective memory assessments with a fair amount of self-awareness. However, many factors influence the accuracy of subjective memory assessments. People who are chronic worriers tend to score themselves lower than people who are eternal optimists. People with higher education tend to score themselves higher than people with less formal education. Additionally, memory assessments need to be adjusted by age. Older people experience more memory problems than younger folks, so scores need to be adjusted accordingly. Finally, one must take into account whether memory problems are the result of not paying attention enough, or real changes in memory. One way to address these variables is by taking the assessments twice, once at the beginning of the *Brainfit* program and once at the end. That way you can measure your personal improvements based on the gains you've achieved through participation in the program.

The categories in the subjective memory test follow the progression of the *Brainfit* workout stations. They also represent the memory areas most people commonly worry about. This assessment requires five to ten minutes to complete. Since the test is based on your own perceptions, it should be completed by you without any help or interference. In evaluating your own memory, how often do the items below present a problem for you. Circle the number (with 1 being no problem and 7 a severe problem) that best reflects your overall judgment about your memory.

How Often Do These Present a Problem For You?

Remembering Who	No Problem					Severe Problem	
Names of people	1	2	3	4	5	6	7
Names of places (e.g., restaurants, stores)	1	2	3	4	5	6	7
Titles (e.g., books, movies)	1	2	3	4	5	6	7

Remembering What							
To complete errands	1	2	3	4	5	6	7
To perform household chores	1	2	3	4	5	6	7
To buy something at the supermarket	1	2	3	4	5	6	7
To finish a task I started	1	2	3	4	5	6	7

Remembering How Many							
Phone numbers I use often	1	2	3	4	5	6	7
Important personal numbers (e.g., license, security codes)	1	2	3	4	5	6	7
How to balance my checkbook	1	2	3	4	5	6	7

Remembering When	No Problem					Severe Problem	
Appointments and meetings	1	2	3	4	5	6	7
Special occasions (e.g., birthdays)	1	2	3	4	5	6	7
To take medications on time	1	2	3	4	5	6	7

Remembering Where							
Where I put things (e.g., keys, TV remote)	1	2	3	4	5	6	7
Where I parked my car	1	2	3	4	5	6	7
Directions to familiar places	1	2	3	4	5	6	7

Remembering in Conversations							
What I was just saying	1	2	3	4	5	6	7
Whether I told someone something	1	2	3	4	5	6	7
Whether someone told me something	1	2	3	4	5	6	7
Finding the right word	1	2	3	4	5	6	7

Interpreting Your Subjective Memory Score

Now that you've completed the subjective memory pre-assessment, it's time to interpret your score, which will represent your average score from 1 to 7. This score is a starting point and provides a way to measure your own progress. In addition to determining your baseline score, note any particular categories in which you are experiencing memory difficulties. These categories represent areas of focus for you in the *Brainfit* program.

Here's how the self-scoring mechanism works:
1. Add up the total score of all the items you circled.
2. Divide your total score by 20 (the total number of items in all the categories)
3. If your average score is:

Score	**Interpretation**
1	You have no perceived memory problems
2–3	You perceive mild memory problems
4–5	You perceive moderate memory problems
6–7	You perceive major memory problems

Write down your subjective memory score, as you will need it in Chapter Eleven to assess your memory improvements.

Objective Memory Pre-Assessment[12]

Now let's try an objective memory pre-assessment. You must read through the list of words just once, and only once, concentrating on each word. Then cover the list and write down as many words as you can remember on a sheet of paper.

Plate	Cry	Queen
Pound	Hip	Dance
Fold	Gift	Shirt
Pile	Apples	Step

How many words did you remember? Write down the number of words you remembered. This will serve as your baseline score for your objective memory assessment. In Chapter Eleven you will take the objective post-memory assessment to assess your memory gains as a result of your participation in the *Brainfit* program.

Interpreting Your Objective Memory Score

The average person aged 18–39 can remember ten items. Ages 40–59 remember, on average, nine items; ages 60–69 remember eight items, and folks 70 and older remember seven items. Do not fret if your score is lower than the average—you will surely boost your score as a result of your participation in the *Brainfit* program. Keep this score, along with your subjective memory score, in a safe place, as you will need them for comparative purposes in Chapter Eleven.

Mental Agility Pre-Assessment

Mental agility tests often are based on inductive and deductive reasoning. The following mental agility pre-assessment asks you to use deductive reasoning or logical reasoning. Deductive reasoning is the process of reaching a conclusion that is guaranteed to follow, if the evidence provided is true and the reasoning used to reach the conclusion is correct. The conclusion must be based only on the evidence previously provided. To complete the mental agility pre-assessment follow the instructions below.

Instructions

The items in each row below form a series. The series is based on a predictable pattern or rule. Fill in the answer that completes each series. For the graphic illustrations, select the letter corresponding to the shape that completes the series. Before you begin, have a piece of scrap paper handy. When you are ready to begin, **set a timer for five minutes.** Stop when the timer goes off. Read the answer key at the end of the chapter and circle the items you answered correctly. How many items did you answer correctly? This is your baseline score. Keep this "score" as you will need it again in Chapter Eleven.

1. 0, ½, 1 ½, 3, 5, 7½, 10 ½, _____

2. Mondale, Bush, Bush, Quayle, _____

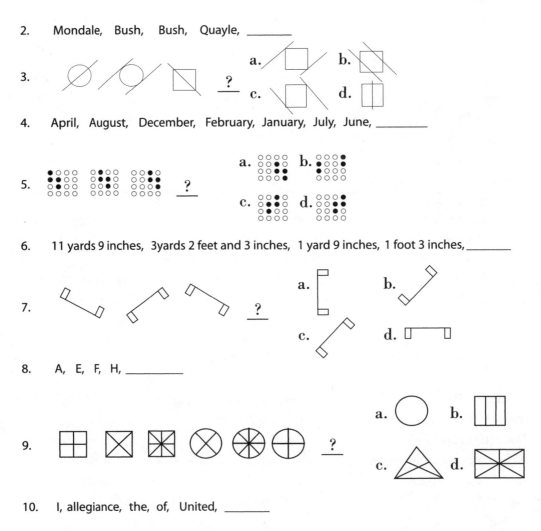

4. April, August, December, February, January, July, June, _____

6. 11 yards 9 inches, 3 yards 2 feet and 3 inches, 1 yard 9 inches, 1 foot 3 inches, _____

8. A, E, F, H, _____

10. I, allegiance, the, of, United, _____

14

Brainy Knowledge Quiz[13]

How much do you know about the miraculous organ we call the brain? Before you begin your *Brainfit* exercise program, take the Brainy Quiz below to see how much you know about the human brain. Circle the correct response, than check your responses in the solutions at the end of this chapter.

1. There is no sense of pain in the brain itself, which explains why neurosurgeons can probe areas of the brain while the patient is still awake.
   a. True
   b. False

2. The consistency of the brain is most like which of the following:
   a. Plastic
   b. Swiss cheese
   c. Warm, wet sponge

3. The adult human brain weighs about:
   a. 10 pounds
   b. 3 pounds
   c. 15 pounds

4. Which mammal has the largest brain in relation to its body size?
   a. Gorilla
   b. Human being
   c. Blue whale

5. Although the brain accounts for only 2 percent of the body's weight, it uses 20 percent of all the oxygen we breathe and gets 20 percent of the blood flow.
   a. True
   b. False

6. During the first month of life, the number of connections between brain cells dramatically increases from 50 trillion to 1 quadrillion. If an infant's body grew at a

comparable rate, its weight would increase from 8.5 pounds at birth to 170 pounds at one month old.
  a. True
  b. False

7. The average adult has approximately how many brain cells?
  a. 10 million
  b. 5 trillion
  c. 100 billion

8. The brain and spinal cord make up the central nervous system
  a. True
  b. False

9. Neurons are nerve cells that send and receive electrochemical signals to and from the brain and nervous system.
  a. True
  b. False

10. Neurons transmit nerve signals to and from the brain at up to:
  a. 60 miles an hour
  b. 100 miles an hour
  c. 200 miles an hour

11. Glial brain cells (glue cells) make up 90 percent of our brain cells. Their primary function is to:
  a. transmit messages between brain cells
  b. provide physical and nutritional support for neurons
  c. stimulate growth of new neurons

12. The right hemisphere of the brain controls:
  a. the right side of the body
  b. the left side of the body
  c. both sides of the body

13. The three major parts of the brain are the cerebrum, the cerebellum, and the
    a. frontal lobe
    b. olfactory bulb
    c. brain stem

14. Scientists believe that every time you have a new thought or memory, you are making a new connection between brain cells.
    a. True
    b. False

15. The average adult permanently loses thousands of brain cells daily.
    a. True
    b. False

16. Brain cells die through a natural process called apoptosis, in which neurons that do not receive or transmit information become damaged or die.
    a. True
    b. False

17. One of the earliest signs of Alzheimer's disease is a degraded sense of:
    a. Hearing
    b. Taste
    c. Smell

18. A study by the Dana Foundation found that nearly seven out of ten adults have concerns about memory loss.
    a. True
    b. False

19. Strokes, or "brain attacks," are the third leading cause of death in the United States. A stroke occurs when the blood flow to the brain is disrupted.
    a. True
    b. False

20. If we do not find a cure for Alzheimer's disease, the number of Americans with Alzheimer's by the year 2050 is estimated to be:
    a. 4 million
    b. 14 million
    c. 44 million

21. Regular mental exercise helps protect against Alzheimer's disease.
    a. True
    b. False

22. The brain is a dynamic organ capable of regeneration.
    a. True
    b. False

23. Albert Einstein's huge intelligence is attributed to:
    a. the size of his brain
    b. the number of his brain cells
    c. the number and complexity of the neural connections between his brain cells

24. By our late twenties the first signs of brain aging can be seen on brain scans.
    a. True
    b. False

25. The brain thrives on:
    a. Routine
    b. Surprise
    c. Novelty

Solutions

Mental Agility Pre-Assessment Answers

1. 14 (increase the first number by the difference between the two successive numbers)
2. Gore (Vice Presidents)
3. c
4. March (months in alphabetical order)
5. b
6. 5 inches (a third of the previous distance)
7. b
8. I (capital letters that can be drawn with straight lines)
9. d
10. Of (every other word in the Pledge of Allegiance)

Brainy Knowledge Quiz Answers

1. True	10. C	19. True
2. C	11. B	20. B
3. B	12. B	21. True
4. B	13. C	22. True
5. True	14. True	23. C
6. True	15. True	24. True
7. C	16. True	25. C
8. True	17. C	
9. True	18. True	

Chapter Two

Making Memories

*"I sometimes worry about my short
attention span, but not for very long."*
—Herb Caen, San Francisco Chronicle,
February 10, 1974

Senior Moments

Amy, an occupational therapist and soccer mom, is in her mid-forties, but she is already worried about what she calls her "senior moments." And she is not alone. A 2005 University of California at San Francisco Web article on memory and aging confirms that "memory loss has long been recognized as a common accompaniment of aging. The inability to recall the name of a recent acquaintance or the contents of a short shopping list are familiar experiences for everyone."[1] Given the fact that memory peaks at about age thirty, this is not so surprising. Still, when you find yourself misplacing your keys, leaving the soup boiling over on the stove, or calling the police to report your car stolen when you've actually just misplaced it in a large parking lot, it is disconcerting to say the very least. Our underlying sense of panic is driven by the fact that memory is not just about an inventory of facts we've learned. Rather it is the recognition that memory is the heart of our identity, holding together the story of our lives. As Oscar Wilde once put it, "Memory . . . is the diary we all carry with us." By protecting our memory, we preserve the scrapbook of our lives.

Why Do We Forget?

Does it sometimes seem like you forget more than you remember? Forgetting, however frustrating, actually has some tangible benefits. Imagine what it would be like if you remembered every minute detail of every hour of every day during your entire life. Consider what it would be like if you had to sort through all those stored details to retrieve important information. Many scientists theorize that forgetting is a natural and important part of brain function that keeps us from being swamped with useless information. Some scientists further speculate that we are physiologically preprogrammed to eventually erase data that is no longer relevant to us, sort of like using the recycle bin on your computer. Finally, there is no such thing as a perfect memory. Forgetting is part of being human.

There are many reasons we forget things, and sometimes these reasons overlap. Some of the most common reasons include lack of attention, distractions, and poor information storage techniques (encoding). One of the most frustrating forgetting scenarios is the tip-of-the-tongue phenomenon. Failing to remember something doesn't mean it is gone forever; in the case of the tip-of-the-tongue phenomenon, we usually remember the forgotten word or phrase in time. Still, it is helpful to have strategies on hand for retrieving forgotten information in the moment. Next time you forget something important, try using one or more of the following retrieval strategies.

Information Retrieval Strategies

1. Relax: Relax and allow your mind to travel through the storage bins in your brain. Anxiety blocks memory functions. Sometimes just relaxing the mind or closing your eyes will bring the word or phrase to consciousness. Also, trust your brain's instincts: if your brain is fixated on a word beginning with the letter *P*, go with the clue. There is probably some relationship between *P* and the word you are seeking. For example, suppose you are trying to remember the name of an acquaintance. You find your brain is stuck on the name Bob, which you know to be wrong. You relax your mind and trust the *B* clue, as if you were playing a game. Names starting with *B* start to float to the surface . . . Bob, Bill, Ben. Suddenly, the correct name, Bart, jumps to the surface and locks into place.

2. Relate: Try and jog your brain by calling up related information. For example, if you are trying to remember the title of a particular movie, remember as many other related facts about the movie as you can: who starred in it, the plot of the film, with whom you saw it. Often one little fact will catapult the missing word or phrase into your mind. Here are several approaches for using the "relate" strategy.[2]

Approach	Explanation
Alphabetic search	Recite the alphabet slowly searching for a first letter connection.
Scenario search	Visualize the scene, the people, and the location where you learned the information.
Association search	Try to see, hear, or touch something that you originally associated with the information.
Chronological search	Retrace your steps mentally in order to locate the moment when you last used the information.
Event search	What were you doing when you used the information?
Visual search	Visualize the paper on which the information was written.
People search	Recall the people with whom you used the information. What did they say, do, or look like?
Increase Stimulus search	Keep listening to the request or ask for more information.

3.   **Research:** To ensure quick retrieval of important information, stay current by reviewing or relearning the needed information. Going to a reunion? Get out your old yearbook and skim through the pictures and articles. Going out to dinner? What topics are likely to come up (e.g., politics, world events, movies, books, sports)? Review key topics and associated facts to ensure comfortable conversation. Research is also a useful tool for relearning information. If you were once fluent in a second language, but can not recall certain words or remember correct grammatical syntax, take a refresher course.

How Does Memory Work?

If you want to tone up your body, it helps to understand the location and nature of the different muscle groups. Likewise, when toning up your memory, it is helpful to understand how memory works. Memory is a complex and fascinating process that continues to intrigue and challenge scientists. Current memory experts generally agree that memories are acquired and secured through three sequential memory processes: **sensory memory, short-term memory,** and **long-term memory.**

There is even a **pre-memory stage** that consists of random, unnoticed sensory stimuli. Suppose you are at the beach reading a book. Unconsciously you are absorbing a myriad of sounds, smells, and tactile feelings. There are waves crashing on the shore, the salty smell of the ocean is in the air, bits of sand are blowing against your skin, seagulls are screeching as they forage for food, children are splashing in the water, people are talking and walking on the boardwalk, radios are blaring from beach blankets, and so on. In pre-memory, we experience these as fleeting sensations without consciousness.

Memory begins in the very brief moment when the mind consciously recognizes what the senses are taking in. We call this sensory memory. For example, you may momentarily look up from your book as your mind registers the sound of a child crying. In most cases, there is no need to record these external sensory experiences, so they are filtered out and discarded.

When, however, sensory impression is paid attention to, it moves to the second stage of memory, which is called short-term memory or working memory. Perhaps your cell phone rings, but you miss the call. You look at the caller identification and see that your mother has called, and make a mental note to call her right back. We can think of short-term memory as the temporary "scratch pad" on which everything that might get committed to long-term memory is temporarily placed. For example, in order to understand this sentence you need to hold in your mind the beginning of the sentence so that you will understand the end. Short-term memory has a limited capacity and time frame for storing and recalling information. If not rehearsed (in other words, repeated and practiced), information in short-term memory may not last longer than thirty seconds. Short-term memory that is not transferred to long-term memory is discarded. When, however, information is consciously rehearsed and organized it moves from short-term memory to long-term memory. Long-term memory is the largest component of the memory system. It can hold information over a lifetime and its storage capacity is limitless.

Encoding and Retrieving Information

There are two important mental activities related to an effective long-term memory. They are **encoding** and **retrieval.** Encoding is the activity of getting information solidly secured in the storage bins of long-term memory. It consists of mental tasks like paying attention, rehearsing information, or associating new learning with information the brain already knows. Suppose you are a lawyer. It is easier for you to remember a new legal statute than to remember the steps in a science experiment because your brain is already familiar with legal data and has previously set up storage bins containing this type of information. Retrieval is the activity of obtaining information from long-term memory when needed. Information that has been solidly encoded and organized in long-term memory is easier to retrieve than information that has been randomly filed.

The act of remembering can be defined as the ability to encode (organize and store) and retrieve learned information. How well you remember is a direct function of the strength and organization of the encoding and retrieval processes. The five fundamental memory skills of **Active Observation, Visualization, Verbalization, Linking,** and **Chunking**, which you will learn about in Chapter Three, will boost your brain's natural encoding and retrieval processes by helping you to systematically organize and arrange information according to memorable structures, associations, patterns, and groupings.

A Quick Overview of Human Memory

Here is a pictorial representation of how memory works.

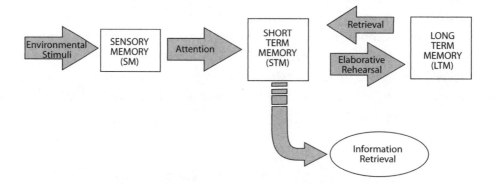

A Quick Summary of Memory Processes

The following chart provides a summary of the three memory processes along with a memory tip for boosting your brain's own memory mechanisms.

Process	Definition	Examples	Memory Tip
Sensory Memory	Environmental stimuli the brain senses	Hearing the sound of a church bell Feeling a raindrop land on your nose	Turn up your sensory antennae; activate all five senses
Short-term Memory	Consciously paying attention to what the senses are taking in, so that you can perform an immediate task	Adding up a column of numbers in your head	Avoid interruptions, distractions, and multi-tasking
Long-term Memory	Learned information stored in the brain for future use	The skill of balancing a checkbook	Connect the information to be remembered to information the brain already knows

Memory Tips for Absentmindedness

When we are tired, stressed, or feeling blue, our memory sometimes short-circuits, and we find ourselves becoming more absentminded. Many people with perfectly good memories occasionally suffer from this annoying memory malfunction. Here are some helpful tips for dealing with absent-mindedness.

1. Put items to be remembered in an unusual place. For example, put letters to be mailed by the front door.
2. Have a "catch-all" memory place. This is a special place for items that you are too busy to put away properly.

3. Organize your environment: a place for everything and everything in its place.

4. Set an alarm or timer to help you remember to do something at a certain time.

5. Keep an updated calendar or datebook.

6. Keep a To Do list.

7. Keep a notepad in your pocket, by your bed, and in your car to capture things you suddenly remember you must do.

8. Use object cues. This is similar to tying a string around your finger. For example, turn your ring or watch around; put a crumpled bill in with your change; tip a lampshade. Noticing something different about the object will remind you that you are supposed to remember something.

9. Write notes to yourself, and post them in conspicuous places.

10. Don't procrastinate. Do it now!

11. Don't multitask. Focus and finish one thing at a time.

12. Count items you need to take with you so you won't leave any behind.

13. Experiment with electronic organizers.

14. Pay attention! You can't remember what you never observed in the first place.

15. Ask a friend or family member to remind you of an important upcoming event.

What's the Workout Rationale?

As you progress through the Brainfit program you will draw on both short-term and long-term memory processes. The following series of daily exercises will give you an opportunity to flex your short-term and long-term memory muscles.

Let's Work Out!

Welcome to the **Making Memories** fitness station. Now that you understand the basics of how memory works, it's time to get those brain cells firing. Each exercise contains instructions, followed by useful feedback. There are four short-term memory exercises followed by three long-term memory exercises.

Weekly Exercise Planner

The following table lays out the *Brainfit* workout for **Making Memories.**

Day	Exercise Name	Skill	Pages
Day One	Jumbles	Short-Term	28–30
Day Two	Short Stories	Short-Term	31–33
Day Three	Shipshape	Short-Term	34–35
Day Four	Mix & Match	Short-Term	36–37
Day Five	Ancient History	Long-Term	38–39
Day Six	Daily Sightings	Long-Term	40
Day Seven	Trivia Games	Long-Term	41–44

Day One: Jumbles

Skill: Short-Term Memory

Number of Exercises: Two

Exercise One

This short-term memory exercise will challenge your memory for recalling random words. The exercise consists of two rounds. In the second round, you'll be given a memory clue to boost your word-recall skills.

Round One

1. Read the first word grouping (row one) out loud.
2. Look away and try to repeat the words in the group.
3. Read the next word grouping out loud.
4. Look away and try and repeat the words in this group.
5. Repeat steps 3 and 4 until you have finished all the word groupings below.
6. Write down the number of words you remember in each row.

dog, banana, bike

apple, diaper, tire, nail

scissors, phone, automobile, paper, cream

golf, operation, math, vacation, rug, laundry

brain, mind, remember, forget, think, know, learn

Which group of words was easiest to remember? Most people say the last group is, even though it is the longest. It is easier to remember a list of items if they have something in common. Find a label or category that connects the items in the last word group. Grouping items by common label boosts information storage and retrieval.

Round Two

Follow the steps in Round One for the new word pyramid that follows. However, this time before you recite a group of words out loud, look for a way to connect all or some of the words in the grouping. For example, in the Round One word pyramid, the first row contains two words that begin with the letter B: *banana*, and *bike*. In row two, the words *nail* and *tire* might be connected by visualizing a nail stuck in a tire, and so on. Use your creativity to find connections among the words. Then read the words in each row out loud, cover the words, and see how many words you can remember.

shovel, computer, clock
snow, flower, zebra, underwear
flute, book, milk, envelope, gum
finger, sweater, box, pill, watermelon, wristwatch
tiger, zoo, food, cage, monkey, children, ticket

How did you do? Was it easy or hard to find word connections? Did you remember more words in Round One or Round Two? Most people can remember more items in a list when they find meaningful connections among the items.

Exercise Two

In Exercise One, your short-term memory was challenged by recalling random words. In Exercise Two, your short-term memory will be challenged by remembering random picture objects. Study the objects in the picture on the next page for no more than two minutes. Then cover the picture jumble and write down the names of all the objects you can remember in the space below.

Was it easier for you to remember jumbled words or jumbled picture objects? What strategy did you use to help you remember the objects? Did you see relationships among the objects that helped you to connect them together in your memory?

Day Two: Short Stories

Skill: Short-Term Memory
Number of Exercises: Two

Exercise One

Below is a brief summary of things you need to do today. Read the summary. Then answer the questions that follow without looking back at the summary. See how many items on your daily To Do list you can remember.

You are meeting your friend, Tom, for lunch at 12:45 P.M. at the Downtown Deli. After lunch, you need to swing by the bank to cash a check. You also need to pick up your shirts at the cleaners. Then, it's off to get your kids, Rachel and Elizabeth, at soccer practice. Elizabeth needs to be dropped off at a friend's birthday party. You and Rachel will then go to the grocery store and pick up a few items for dinner. You are making macaroni and cheese for dinner. Your wife, Susan, should be home from her business meeting at around 9:00 P.M. After the kids go to bed, you'll read your e-mail and respond to your voice mail. If you're lucky, you and Susan will have an hour to relax and catch up on the news of the day.

Questions

1. What do you need to do at the bank? _____

2. What are your children's names? _____

3. Where do you need to pick up your children? _____

4. Why are you going to the grocery store? _____

5. Who needs to go to a birthday party? _____

6. What do you need to pick up at the cleaners? _____

7. What are you making for dinner? _____

8. What is your wife's name? _____

9. Why isn't your wife home for dinner? _____

10. Where are you meeting your friend for lunch? _____

11. What is your friend's name? _____

12. What time are you meeting your friend? _____

13. What time will your wife be home? _____

14. What will you do after the kids go to bed? _____

15. What will you and Susan discuss at the end of the day? _____

16. How does Elizabeth get home from the birthday party? _____

If you missed any questions, go back and read the summary again. See if you can remember more items after a second reading. Did you find the trick question (16)? Try the same memory fitness exercise substituting a magazine article or newspaper story. Ask a friend to read the article first and make up several questions. Then read the article yourself and answer the questions.

Exercise Two

Read the short stories below, then cover the stories and answer the questions that follow. After you have answered the questions, reread the stories to check your answers.

The Cash Register Story

A businessman just turned off the lights in the store when a man appeared and demanded money. The owner opened a cash register. The contents of the cash register were scooped up, and the man sped away. A member of the police force was notified promptly.

Questions

1. The man who opened the cash register was the owner. True or False?

2. A man appeared after the owner had turned off his store lights. True or False?

3. The robber was a man. True or False?

4. The story contains a series of events in which only four persons are referred to: the owner of the store, a man who demanded money, and two members of the police force. True or False?

The Car Chase

A red BMW sped around the courthouse, pursued by a black Mercedes. It screeched through a traffic light that was just turning red, barely missing an old man crossing the street who was carrying a cane and a bag of groceries. Coming from the opposite direction was a police car with lights flashing and sirens blaring. The BMW swerved to avoid the police car, but the Mercedes slammed into a fire hydrant, which began spurting water, much to the delight of the neighborhood children.

Questions

1. Which direction was the police car coming from? _____

2. How many items did the old man have in tow? _____

3. What color was the traffic light? _____

4. Which car hit the fire hydrant? _____

How well did you remember the details in the police stories? What helped you remember the details? For instance, did you read more slowly, rehearse the details in your mind, or visualize the events? Stories with emotional content, like those involving crimes, are easier to remember than stories without emotional content.

Day Three: Shipshape

Skill: Short-Term Memory
Number of Exercises: Two

Exercise One

In yesterday's exercises, you practiced remembering written information in a meaningful story context. Today, you'll try your hand at remembering visual information presented in a random context.[3]

Copy the design as accurately as you can in the space below. At the top of the next page draw the design again from memory. How do the designs compare? For extra challenge, put the design copies aside. Try to redraw the design after a thirty minute break.

How did you do? What strategy did you use to give meaning to the abstract shapes so that you might remember them better? When drawing from recall, the typical person will get the basic outline and 25 to 50 percent of the details.

Exercise Two

Give yourself five seconds to commit each symbol to memory. Cover the symbols and draw as many as you can remember. Repeat the process on a seprarate piece of paper from the start five times.[4] To reduce the level of difficulty, work on one line at a time.

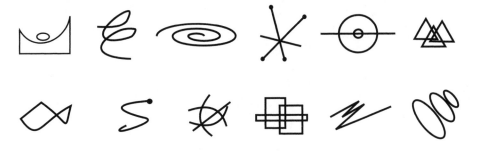

Did your memory slowly improve with repetition? What strategy did you use to help you remember? Linking a symbol to an image the brain already knows can boost memory recall. For instance, an abstract symbol may remind you of a star or curly piece of hair.

Day Four: Mix & Match

Skill: Short-Term Memory
Number of Exercises: One

Exercise One

In this exercise, you will be asked to recall the numbers associated with a set of shapes. The exercise consists of two rounds: a rehearsal round, and a recall round. [5]

Round One: Rehearsal

Take a look at the shapes and their associated numbers. Try to remember the number that goes with each shape. Then cover up the numbers and shapes and proceed to Round Two.

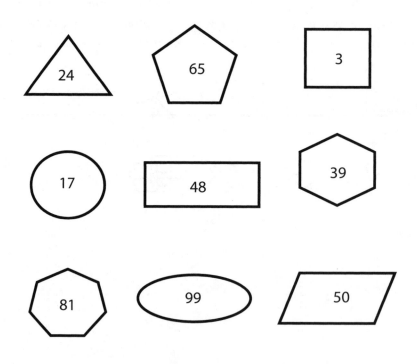

Round Two: Recall

From recall, try to match each number with its corresponding shape. Write the correct number in each shape.

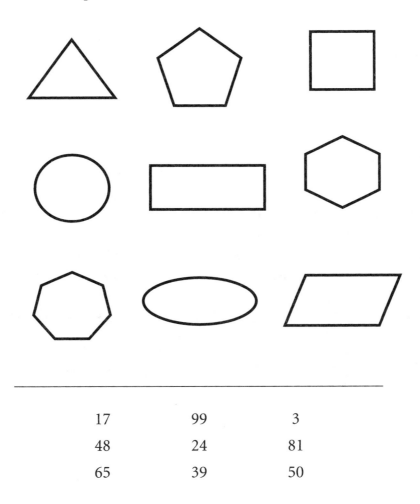

17	99	3
48	24	81
65	39	50

How did you do? What technique did you use to link the numbers with the shapes. In Chapter Six, "Remembering How Many," you will learn how to turn numbers into shapes that can be linked to other shapes.

Day Five: Ancient History
Skill: Long-Term Memory
Number of Exercises: Three

Workout Introduction

Dr. Endel Tulving's model of human memory proposes three types of long-term memory: **semantic** (general world knowledge), **episodic** (personally experienced events), and **procedural** (learned skills).[6] Interestingly, people with amnesia usually forget personal information, but retain general world knowledge. Challenge your long-term memory by trying to recall information in each of the three memory categories.

Exercise One: Semantic Memory

To give your long-term memory a stretch, answer the questions below. Not sure? Stretch your brain by proactively seeking the answers. While researching the answers to these questions, try to learn three new facts. Check your answers at the end of the chapter.

1. Name the last five presidents of the United States. _____

_____

2. Name the six New England states. _____

_____

3. In which country is the Taj Mahal located? _____

4. What are the words to the American national anthem? _____

_____

5. In which country were the 2005 winter Olympics held? _____

6. Name three movies in which Julia Roberts starred. _____

_____

7. Name the oceans of the world. _____

_____

8. Which countries border Iraq? _____

_____

Exercise Two: Episodic Memory

See how many of these personally experienced events you can recall. Get together with family members to see if they remember these personal events the same way you do.

1. What was the name of your first grade teacher? _____

2. Who was your first romantic heartbreak? _____

3. What was the naughtiest thing you did as a child? _____

4. Who was your best friend in grade school? _____

5. Where were you when you lost your first tooth? _____

6. What did your maternal grandfather do for a living? _____

7. What was your favorite television show in elementary school? _____

8. What was your favorite toy or stuffed animal as a child? _____

9. What color was your first bicycle? _____

Exercise Three: Procedural Memory

Could you teach someone the procedures for executing a familiar task from memory? Pick one of the following tasks and write down the step-by-step procedures for how to do the task. Do not look up the instructions; go by memory alone. Imagine that your audience is someone who has never performed the task before. Then get someone who has never performed the task to follow your instructions exactly without asking questions.

a. Make a favorite recipe _____

b. Change a flat tire _____

c. Balance a checkbook _____

d. Check the oil fluid level in a car _____

e. Hook up a DVD player _____

f. Create an Excel spreadsheet on the computer _____

How did your procedural memory and instructions hold up?

Day Six: Daily Sightings

Skill: Long-Term Memory
Number of Exercises: One

Exercise One

Below are some things you see or do on a regular basis. See how many of these every-day items you have absorbed and can retrieve from long-term memory. If helpful, close your eyes and use your visualization skills. Check your answers at the end of the chapter.

1. On a touch-tone telephone keypad, where is the ✳ located? _____

2. To open the flow of water on a garden spigot (faucet), do you turn the knob to the left or the right? _____

3. If you are parallel parking on the right side of the street, do you begin by turning your wheel to the right or the left? _____

4. On a standard computer keyboard how many rows of letters are there? _____

5. What is the order of the colors on a traffic light from top to bottom? _____

6. Is the bread plate to the right or left of the dinner plate? _____

7. To exit a public building do you push the door? _____

8. Draw the symbol printed on a handicapped parking sign.

9. How many R's are on a railroad crossing sign? _____

10. What is the license plate number (letters/word) on your car? _____

11. In the alphabet, what is the last uppercase letter printed without a straight line? _____

12. How many red stripes are on an American flag? _____

Day Seven: Trivia Games

Skill: Long-Term Memory
Number of Exercises: One

Exercise One

There are lots of variations of trivia games on the market that challenge your long-term memory. The following trivia exercise consists of two rounds. The questions are the same in each round, however, the format changes. The first round asks you to *recall* information from long-term memory without prompts. The second round asks you to *recognize* information using multiple-choice prompts.

Round One: Recalling Information

Try to *recall* the answers to the following trivia questions. Write your answers in the space provided below each question.

1. Who played Rhett Butler in the movie epic
   Gone with the Wind? _____

2. What is the capital of New York? _____

3. Who played Rose (female lead) in the movie
   Titanic? _____

4. What is the name of Judy Garland's famous
   daughter? _____

5. Who is known as the "King of Pop"? _____

6. What is the national bird of the United States? _____

7. What famous World War II general later became
   president of the United States? _____

8. Who was vice president under the late President
   Ronald Reagan? _____

9. What is the name of the popular herbal remedy
   for boosting memory? _____

10. What is the name of the chemistry chart that shows a tabular arrangement of the elements according to their atomic number? _____

11. What is the name of the metabolic disorder for which people take insulin? _____

12. Who wrote the play *The Taming of the Shrew*? _____

13. What famous baseball player had a disease named after him? _____

Round Two: Recognizing Information

Here is the exercise again in a different format. This format asks you to *recognize* the correct answer from a multiple-choice list. Circle the correct response. Check your answers at the end of the chapter.

1. Who played Rhett Butler in the movie epic *Gone with the Wind*?
   a. Clark Kent
   b. Humphrey Bogart
   c. Clark Gable
   d. Jimmy Stewart

2. What is the capital of New York?
   a. Buffalo
   b. New York City
   c. Albany
   d. Syracuse

3. Who played Rose (the female lead) in the movie *Titanic*?
   a. Cate Blanchett
   b. Gwyneth Paltrow
   c. Kate Winslet
   d. Helena Bonham Carter

4. What is the name of Judy Garland's famous daughter?
   a. Audrey Hepburn
   b. Eliza Tillman
   c. Kate Hudson
   d. Liza Minnelli

5. Who is known as the "King of Pop"?
   a. Elvis Presley
   b. The Beatles
   c. Ricky Martin
   d. Michael Jackson

6. What is the United States' national bird?
   a. turkey
   b. spotted owl
   c. pink flamingo
   d. bald eagle

7. What famous World War II general later became president of the United States?
   a. Norman Schwarzkopf
   b. George S. Patton, Jr.
   c. Dwight D. Eisenhower
   d. Douglas MacArthur

8. Who was vice president under the late President Ronald Reagan?
   a. George H. W. Bush
   b. Dan Quayle
   c. Al Gore
   d. Gerald R. Ford

9. What is the name of the popular herbal remedy for boosting memory?
   a. zinc glutamate
   b. ginkgo biloba
   c. remefemin
   d. echinacea

10. What is the name of the chemistry chart that shows a tabular arrangement of the elements according to their atomic number?
    a. Atomic Formula Table
    b. Elemental Table of Chemistry
    c. Periodic Table of Elements
    d. The Elements and Their Atomic Numbers

11. What is the name of the metabolic disorder for which people take insulin?
    a. thyroid imbalance
    b. folic acid deficiency
    c. endocrine imbalance
    d. diabetes

12. Who wrote the play *The Taming of the Shrew*?
    a. Molière
    b. William Shakespeare
    c. Neil Simon
    d. Anton Chekhov

13. What famous baseball player had a degenerative disease named after him?
    a. Babe Ruth
    b. Ted Williams
    c. Mickey Mantle
    d. Lou Gehrig

Which version of the exercise was easier, *recall* or *recognition*? Most people find recalling information more difficult than recognizing it. Free recall is challenging because the brain has to search through long-term memory storage bins without the aid of any retrieval clues.

In case you weren't sure of the correct responses, they are at the end of the chapter.

Dr. Brainfit's Advice Column

Dear Dr. Brainfit,

When I had a test to study for and I couldn't concentrate, my mother would tell me to run around the block three times. She said it would make me smarter. Is there any truth to this?

Janine from Dallas

Dear Janine,

Your mother gave you good advice.

Aerobic Exercise and the Brain

Physical activity and aerobic exercise do good things for mood and memory. Scientists have known for a long time that physical exercise increases the circulation of **endorphins**—hormones released in our brains after exercise that have been shown to elevate mood and memory. Research studies show a definite link between aerobic exercise and brain strength. New studies, involving laboratory animals, suggest that physical exercise may lead to the growth of new brain cells and new neural connections. Additionally, aerobic exercise increases blood circulation to the brain, which brings with it oxygen and other nutrients needed for brain health. These brain-healthy changes, scientists speculate, might help stave off Alzheimer's disease. University of Illinois researchers using high-tech neuro-imaging equipment observed that physical activity changes the brain's structure and function in ways that improve attention and decision-making. So even when you don't have a test to study for, it makes good brain sense to keep exercising.

Solutions

Day 5, Exercise One: 1) George W. Bush, Bill Clinton, George H. W. Bush, Ronald Reagan, Jimmy Carter; 2) Maine, Vermont, New Hampshire, Massachusetts, Rhode Island, Connecticut; 3) Agra, Uttar Pradesh, India; 4) Oh say can you see by the dawn's early light; 5) Singapore; 6) *Pretty Woman, Erin Brockovich, Steel Magnolias;* 7) Indian, Atlantic, Pacific, Arctic, Southern; 8) Iran, Kuwait, Syria, Saudi Arabia, Jordan.

Day Six, Exercise One: 1) lower left, 2) left, 3) right, 4) three, 5) red, yellow, green, 6) left, 7) push out, 8) ♿ 9) two, 10) ___, 11) S, 12) seven

Day Seven, Exercise One: 1) Clark Gable, 2) Albany, 3) Kate Winslet, 4) Liza Minnelli, 5) Michael Jackson, 6) bald eagle, 7) Dwight D. Eisenhower, 8) George H. W. Bush, 9) Ginkgo Biloba, 10) Periodic Table of Elements, 11) diabetes, 12) William Shakespeare, 13) Lou Gehrig

Chapter Three

Taking AIM

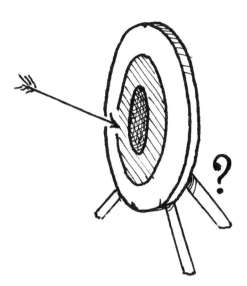

"It is not so astonishing, the number of things I can remember, as the number of things I can remember that aren't so."
—Mark Twain

Taking AIM

Throughout the works of Socrates and Plato, there are references to the golden robed goddess of memory, Mnemosyne. In Greek mythology her union with Zeus, king of the gods, produced the nine muses who presided over all of the arts and sciences. Memory, or Mnemosyne, was honored above all goddesses; for it was believed that memory was the source of all speech, learning, and knowledge. Socrates described memory as a gift from Mnemosyne and likened it to a block of wax that resides in our souls. He taught ". . . that whenever we wish to remember anything we see or hear or think of in our own minds, we hold this wax under the perceptions and thoughts and imprint them upon it, just as we make impressions from seal rings." For Socrates, memory was not the brain or the heart, but the very soul of our existence.

In early Roman and Greek societies immersed in the oral tradition, it was recognized that unless history and traditions were learned by memory and passed on orally, whole cultures might vanish. If memory did not preserve it, the narrated history of an entire nation might vanish without a trace. For singing minstrels and politicians alike, memory was both an art and a science. Many of the memory devices used today are direct descendants of memory systems designed to help ancient Greek politicians make speeches. The AIM memory principle incorporates the fundamentals of memory known since Roman times . . . fundamentals that are as powerful today as they were in ancient times. In fact, AIM is itself a memory device or mnemonic that stands for **attention, imagery,** and **meaning**. Using this mnemonic will help you remember the ABC's of memory enhancement and boost your ability to take aim at important memory targets.

The "A" in AIM = Attention

Does this sound familiar? You pull into the driveway and make a mad dash for the house. You have to go to the bathroom, the ice cream is melting in the grocery bag, and the dog is whining at the back door to be let out. The kids, whom you've left in the car, have to get to soccer practice in five minutes. You attend to your bathroom needs, put the melting ice cream in the freezer, and let the dog out. You hear the car horn honking signaling time is up. . . . But, where did you put those car keys? The "A" in AIM is for attention. You can't remember what you don't pay attention to in the first place. Ever heard the term *multitasking?* It means attending to several tasks in tandem, rather than starting and finishing one before moving on to the next. It is considered a survival strategy and badge of honor in our complex and over-scheduled twenty-first century lives. But recent research suggests that multitasking decreases rather than increases efficiency over the long run. It also is a root cause of memory absentmindedness.

The "I" in AIM = Imagery

Sigmund Freud once said if you want to remember better, make the information you want to remember more interesting. Which is more likely to pique your interest . . . a man on a street corner strumming a guitar or a marching band passing by? Most people would choose the band. It is bright, noisy, and dynamic. It provides a host of sensory input and colorful imagery that grab our attention and imprint on our memory. So, it follows that if we want to remember better, we'll want to create strong visual images that add color, texture, and movement to the things we want to remember.

The "M" in AIM = Meaning

Things that have personal or emotional meaning have more memory impact than things without these connections. Take, for example, your memory of where you were when you first learned that President Kennedy had been shot, or that Princess Diana was in a fatal car crash. Events like these, with their strong personal and emotional impact, are forever etched into our individual and collective memories. If we want to remember better, we need to connect items to be remembered with familiar, personal, and/or emotional meaning.

How AIM Works

The following is an excerpt from the famous novel *The Old Man and the Sea* by Ernest Hemingway. As you read it, pay attention to how Hemingway uses the AIM principle to create an unforgettable memory of the old man. Then answer the questions that follow.

"The Old Man and the Sea"

The old man was thin and gaunt with deep wrinkles in the back of his neck. The brown blotches of the benevolent skin cancer the sun brings from its reflection on the tropic sea were on his cheeks. The blotches ran well down the sides of his face and his hands had the deep-creased scars from handling heavy fish on the cords. But none of these scars were fresh. They were as old as erosions in a fishless desert. Everything about him was old except his eyes and they were the same color as the sea and were cheerful and undefeated.[1]

AIM Analysis

1. What physical features of the old man does the narrator direct to our *attention (A)?*
2. What colorful *images (I)* do the narrator create that stand out in your mind?
3. Provide an example of how the narrator creates *meaning (M)* by associating features of the old man's face to familiar images from nature.

AIM and the Five Memory Skills

Memory experts have identified five memory skills that make using AIM in everyday memory situations easy and fun. These five memory skills create strong memory tracers that boost the brain's own memory acquisition, storage, and retrieval processes. Below is a chart that summarizes the relationship between AIM and the five mental skills of memory.

AIM Memory Skill Definition

AIM	Memory Skill	Definition
Attention	Active Observation	Use your five senses to take in the details of the world around you.
Imagination	Visualization	Create vivid and wacky mental images of what you want to remember.
	Verbalization	Weave what you want to remember into a rhyme or story.
Meaning	Linking	Connect what you want to remember to information the brain already knows.
	Chunking	Group items to be remembered into meaning categories.

Memory Tips for Storing and Retrieving Information

1. Your mind is like a library. Information stored in a meaningful way is easier to retrieve later.
2. Information that is organized is easier for the brain to learn, store, and recall. Organize new information using meaningful hierarchies, groupings, relationships, and patterns.
4. Visual learners will remember best using mental images; auditory learners will remember best using sound cues; kinesthetic learners will remember best by actively using the information.

5. Use the AIM principle (Attention, Imagery, Meaning) to make information more interesting and memorable.

6. Use the five memory skills (Active Observation, Visualization, Verbalization, Linking, and Chunking) to create strong memory storage and retrieval cues.

7. The brain filters out 99 percent of the sensory stimuli it receives through the five senses of sight, sound, smell, taste, and touch.

8. Two factors strongly influence whether or not incoming sensory stimuli is paid attention to and enters into short-term memory:

   a. Information that has meaning, and

   b. Information that has an emotional component or hook.

9. Short-term memory is easily hindered by disruptions that come from multitasking.

10. If information is to move from short-term memory to long-term memory it must be rehearsed.

11. For most people, information must be rehearsed a minimum of three times before it can move from short-term memory to long-term memory.

12. There are two major types of rehearsal strategies:

   a. Rote Rehearsal—deliberate, continuous repetition of material in the same form in which it entered short-term memory.

   b. Elaborative Rehearsal—elaborating or integrating information by giving it some meaningful memory hooks.

13. Many scientists and memory experts contend that there is no such thing as a photographic memory. Instead, they believe people with superior memories use powerful memory strategies.

14. The brain is a network. Memory and thought are contained in patterns of activation in the neural connections between brain cells.

15. Engaging in mentally stimulating activities and exercises activates and strengthens brain connections.

What's the Workout Rationale?

If you want to be a better dancer, golfer, musician, singer, or gymnast, what do you do? You practice, practice, and practice some more. The fundamentals of acquiring skill proficiency remain the same regardless of the discipline. You learn the fundamentals, practice the basics through repetition, then refine and hone your skills by applying them in more complex and challenging situations. Eventually, the skills become part of your "muscle memory" and execution feels natural. Memory is a mental skill that can be practiced and strengthened through a similar process. In this week's workout, "Taking AIM," you will practice using the five memory skills of Active Observation, Visualization, Verbalization, Linking, and Chunking.

Let's Work Out!

Welcome to the **Taking AIM** fitness station. The following series of daily brain fitness exercises will sharpen your ability to take AIM at important memory targets using the five memory skills. Each of the daily exercises is preceded by a skill introduction and provides examples of skill use. The introduction is followed by the daily, ten-minute workout exercises.

Weekly Exercise Planner

The following table lays out the *Brainfit* workout exercises for **Taking AIM**. Each day's workout exercise(s) will be preceded by an Exercise Introduction, which previews the memory skills to be used for the day, and provides examples of how the skills will be applied in the exercises.

Day	Exercise Name	Skill	Pages
Day One	Sense-sational	Active Observation	53–55
Day Two	Hide & Seek	Active Observation	56–58
Day Three	Picture This	Visualization	59–61
Day Four	Rhythm & Rhyme	Verbalization	62–65
Day Five	Hot Connections	Linking	66–67
Day Six	Acronyms & Acrostics	First-Letter Linking	68–72
Day Seven	Bite-Size Pieces	Chunking	73–75

Day One: Sense-sational
Skill: Active Observation
Number of Exercises: Two

Paying attention is the number one factor in cultivating a good memory. In fact, a lot of people blame memory problems for what is really a lack of attention. Activating our five senses will not only help us to pay better attention, it will also create strong memory tracers for storing and retrieving information.

Example One

Elizabeth parks in the underground parking garage of a busy city mall. To be sure she will find her car later, she engages in *active observation*. First, she notes that all the support pillars in her section of the garage are painted blue. Using her imagination, she thinks about how blue she will be if she can't find her car. Her particular row in the blue section is row "R." This makes her think of the phrase "Where R you?" She proceeds to the elevator. A sign on the wall indicates she is on Level 3. She repeats out loud "blue, R, 3." Upon exiting the elevator, she looks for the nearest large anchor store. Located four stores down and to her left is Nordstrom. In front of Nordstrom's is a water pond, with a fountain spraying water and large gold fish swimming about. She also recognizes that she must be near the food court, since she can smell an array of foods. By employing active observation and a little imagination, Elizabeth feels confident she will find her car hours later by retracing her memory markers.

Example Two

Tom travels for a living. Due to airline delays, he often gets into his hotel room late at night and must be up early the next morning. Typically blurry eyed and in a rush, he often wastes precious time in the morning searching for his rental car keys, cell phone, wrist watch, or door swipe card. Of course these items turn up eventually, but always it seems in a surprise location. Sometimes he finds a misplaced item in the bathroom, other times it is on top of the TV console. Once he left the room key in the mini-bar. On the plane ride home, Tom's business associate offers some friendly advice. "Tom, you need to pay more attention. You've got the same problem at work. Hotel rooms all have certain room features in common. Pick a common location that is in every hotel room in every city in the world, and always leave your stuff in the same location. Personally, I put my stuff in a bathroom glass because I know things won't slip off onto the floor. I leave the glass on the nightstand by my bed."

Exercise One

A primary difference between artists and the rest of the population is their ability to see the world through all five senses and to capture these sensory images in art form. Read the following excerpt of a poem by T. S. Eliot twice. As you read the poem, imagine you are walking in the street scene depicted in the poem. Actively observe how the five senses of sight, touch, sound, smell, and taste are used to create strong sensory images and memories. Then answer the questions that follow.

Preludes by T. S. Eliot [2]

The winter evening settles down
With smell of steaks in passageways.
Six o'clock
The burnt-out ends of smoky days.
And now a gusty shower wraps
The grimy scraps
Of withered leaves about your feet
And newspapers from vacant lots;
The showers beat
On broken blinds and chimney pots,
And at the corner of the street
A lonely cab-horse steams and stamps,
And then the lighting of the lamps.

Questions

Try to first answer the questions without looking back at the poem. Then, should you need to, feel free to go back and reread the poem. Don't worry about getting the answers right. Poetry is open to interpretation.

1. What is the primary mood of the poem? _____

2. How does it make you feel? _____

3. What images contribute to this feeling?_____

4. What are some strong smells described in the poem?_____

5. What are some things your body might feel? _____

6. What are some things you might hear? _____

Exercise Two

Often we travel through our daily lives unaware of the world around us. A major reason for this is that we are often lost in our thoughts. We are rarely, if ever, fully present. Today, take a brief walk along a familiar route. Try to empty your mind of mental chatter. Actively observe everything around you. Capture the scene in your mind as T. S. Eliot might. When you get home write down five things you saw or heard that you never really noticed before.

Five New Things I Noticed

1. _____

2. _____

3. _____

4. _____

5. _____

Day Two: Hide & Seek
Skill: Active Observation
Number of Exercises: Three

Have you ever heard the expression, "He can't see the forest for the trees"? Some people see the details and miss the big picture, while others see the big picture and miss the details. In the next three exercises, you'll use active observation once again to observe both the details and the big picture.

Exercise One
Study the movie scene for twenty seconds, then cover the picture and answer the following questions.

1. What food is pictured in the scene? _____

2. What are the oldest and youngest person doing? _____

3. What kind of jewelry are the women wearing? _____

4. How many males and females are in the scene? _____

5. How many people are wearing glasses? _____

6. What other details can you remember? _____

How did you do? For another challenge, try the same exercise with a picture in a book or magazine. Ask a friend to make up questions. How many details can you remember?

Exercise Two

What's wrong with this picture? See if you can find the ten details that are inappropriate, then check your answers against the solution at the end of the chapter.

_____

_____

_____

_____

_____

Exercise Three

The picture below shows an assortment of objects, most of which appear twice but *three* of which appear only once. Look through the assortment of objects until you have identified the three objects which are shown only once. Do not circle these objects. Rather, keep them in your short-term memory. When you believe you have identified all the single objects go back and circle them. Check your answers at the end of the chapter.

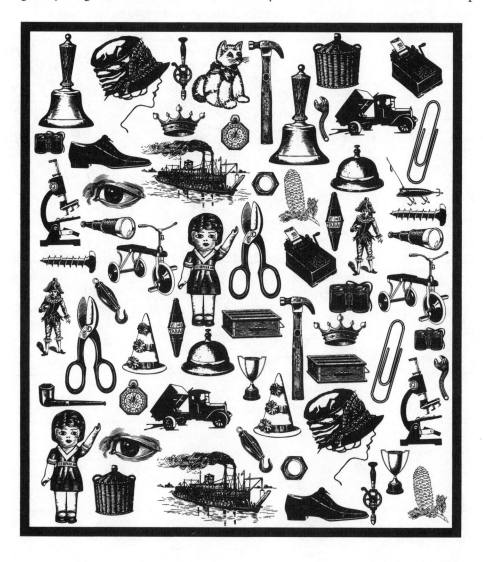

Day Three: Picture This
Skill: Visualization
Number of Exercises: Three

Sixty percent of the population learns best through visual images. For these visual learners, "a picture is worth a thousand words" when it comes to remembering information. As you look at the examples below notice how colorful and wacky the visual images are that are used to boost memory.

Example One

Elizabeth wants to save time and money by purchasing her textbooks online for her college courses. Elizabeth's roommate tells her that a lot of kids are purchasing their text books on *www.amazon.com*. To help her remember this Web site, Elizabeth visualizes her computer in the middle of the Amazon jungle surrounded by scholarly gorillas in professorial robes reading college books.

Example Two

On the way home from work, Chris remembers he forgot to cancel his dentist's appointment. If he doesn't cancel, he will be charged. To remind himself to cancel his appointment when he gets home, Chris pictures a giant, red toothbrush in the shape of a soldier standing guard at his front door.

Example Three

Audrey's daughter remembers best when information to be remembered is presented visually. So Audrey leaves her daughter the following visual message.

Message: Listen for the baby.

Exercise One

Create wild and wacky visual images to help you remember the items below. Use words to describe your image.

1. You want to remember to go to the Red Cross blood drive at your office.

2. You need to remember to call the doctor's office to schedule your fall allergy shots.

3. You need to remember to pick up your tuxedo at the cleaners.

Exercise Two

Create a picture-symbol message to help you remember to perform the following tasks.

1. Take out the trash before noon.

2. Bring the mail in before it rains.

3. Give the dog the heartworm pill.

4. Buy flowers for your administrative assistant.

Exercise Three

Visual memory is a very powerful and underutilized tool for learning and recalling information. In this exercise you'll experiment with learning a list first without the aid of visualization, and then with the aid of visualization.

Round One

You have twenty seconds to memorize the names of the Seven Deadly Sins below. At the end of twenty seconds, cover the list and write down all the sins you can remember.

Pride _____   _____

Lust

Gluttony _____   _____

Anger

Envy _____   _____

Sloth

Greed _____   _____

Round Two

Create a vivid visual image to go with each of the deadly sins. If possible combine two sins in one image. Study the sins and their corresponding images for twenty seconds. Then cover all the information and list as many sins as you can remember.

Sin	Image
Pride	*A politician with a puffed-out chest, red cheeks, and a smug smile.*
Lust	_____
Gluttony	_____
Anger	_____
Envy	_____
Sloth	_____
Greed	_____

Note: Most people remember more words the second time as a result of additional exposure and visual memory hooks.

Day Four: Rhythm & Rhyme

Skill: Verbalization
Number of Exercises: Three

About 40 percent of the population is predominantly verbal. They learn and remember best through auditory means. Auditory learners remember best through the use of rhymes, songs, catch phrases, and repetition.

Example One

The following are examples of common rhymes and catch phrases used to help us remember information.

Water will freeze
At 32 degrees

Red sky at night, sailor's delight
Red sky in the morning, sailors take warning

Example Two

To remember to pick up candles, cake, hot fudge, and ice cream for her son's birthday party, Michelle makes up the following childlike rhyme.

Candles, cake, hot fudge and ice cream
When I bring in dessert the kids will scream

Example Three

Jack needs to stop at the office supply store to pick up the following items for his boss: computer paper, a box of paper clips, twelve CD-ROM disks, a new desk calendar, and color ink cartridges. He doesn't feel the need to write down the items as the list is short and familiar. As he drives to the store he hears "The Twelve Days of Christmas" on the radio. For fun, he finds himself singing along, substituting the office supply items for the actual lyrics. Here are Jack's new lyrics to the tune of "The Twelve Days of Christmas."

On the first day of Christmas, my boss asked me to buy
A ream of computer paper.

On the second day of Christmas, my boss asked me to buy
A box of paper clips,
And a ream of computer paper.

On the third day of Christmas, my boss asked me to buy
Twelve CD-ROM disks,
A box of paper clips,
And a ream of computer paper.

On the fourth day of Christmas, my boss asked me to buy
A new desk calendar,
Twelve CD-ROM disks,
A box of paper clips,
And a ream of computer paper.

On the fifth day of Christmas, my boss asked me to buy
Color ink cartridges,
A new desk calendar,
Twelve CD-ROM disks,
A box of paper clips,
And a ream of computer paper.

The type of cumulative repetition used in "The Twelve Days of Christmas" is similar to the repetition used in many children's memory games. In these games, someone picks a topic like "I'm going on a picnic and I will take . . ." Then in turn each person adds a new item he will take on the picnic. Before adding a new item, however, each person must repeat all of the previously mentioned items in order. This game can be elevated to an adult level simply by picking a more sophisticated topic. It provides a great memory workout for long car rides.

Exercise One

Read each rhyme out loud twice, then cover the rhyme and answer the questions.

Thirty days hath September,
April, June and November;
All the rest have thirty-one,
Except the second month
Which has but twenty-eight in time,
'Til leap year brings it twenty-nine.

1. How many months have thirty days? _____
2. Name three months which have thirty-one days. _____
3. How many days in February in a leap year? _____

If his face is red, raise his head,
If his face is pale, raise his tail.

If someone is unconscious and his face lacks color, after calling 911, what should you do?

_____

Exercise Two

Complete each rhyme below to help you remember important information.

1. **Information:** Your old car is parked on the gold level of the parking garage.

   Rhyme: *My car is _____, I'm parked on _____.*

2. **Information:** At the end of the late news on TV, you must remember to turn off the front porch light.

   Rhyme: *If I don't turn off the _____, my spouse and I will have a _____.*

3. **Information:** You have to be on time for your business meeting in Conference Room A.

    Rhyme: *My business meeting is in Conference Room* _____. *I must hurry and*   *not* _____.

Exercise Three

Ever wonder how the servers at Starbucks can remember each customized order in a matter of seconds? It appears to be an amazing feat. However they are using a proven verbal memory technique. The servers memorize each special order quickly because they use the same repetitive sequence again and again. Here is the repetitive sequence they use:

- Size (e.g., tall, *grande, venti*)
- Decaf (if caffeinated this item is skipped)
- Shots (number of shots of espresso)
- Syrup (e.g., vanilla, hazelnut, etc.)
- Milk (e.g., skim, whole, blended [blended is 2 percent])
- Drink (e.g., iced latte)

If you are a Starbucks coffee drinker, repeat this sequence several times out loud inserting the ingredients in your favorite Starbucks coffee drink. Then cover the sequence and try to place an order for a new custom drink, using the same sequence. Then go to Starbucks and order the drink.

Note: This is a very helpful business technique for customer service representatives who must collect the same items of information from each customer.

Day Five: Hot Connections
Skill: Linking
Number of Exercises: Three

To make the information you want to remember more meaningful, link new information with information the brain already knows. Use a memorable mental picture or story to link items. Personal and emotional links create the strongest memory tracers.

Example One
Keesha has to select a password she will not forget for her new business e-mail, and that will be difficult for someone else at the office to figure out. The person she e-mails most frequently is her sales representative, who is always traveling on the road. Thinking of this connection, she selects *roadsale* for her e-mail password.

Example Two
Mr. Antonelli has to take a bus to his friend's new apartment. His friend tells him to get off at Eightieth Street and Central Boulevard. Mr. Antonelli connects the "eighty" with his age, since he is in his eighties. He links Central Boulevard to his friend's important and *central* position in his life.

Example Three
To remember to pick up toothpaste, aspirin, chewing gum, and hairspray at the pharmacy, Jenny links the words together into this colorful story . . .

*A woman walks into the **pharmacy**. Her hair is puffy and sticky with **hairspray**. She is chomping loudly on a piece of **gum**. Her teeth are yellow and in need of **toothpaste**. When the store clerk looks at her, he gets a headache and needs to take some **aspirin**.*

Exercise One
Imagine you need to select a password for your private Internet chat room, which none of your friends or family will guess. What personally meaningful six- to eight-letter word will you choose for your password?

Exercise Two

Imagine that you've been asked to select both numbers and letters for your new license plate—up to six digits long. What numbers and letters might you select that would have personal meaning for you?

Next, look at the actual letters and numbers on your license plate or that of a family member or friend. Try to memorize the license plate by coming up with familiar links for the numbers and letters. Below is an example of how the license plate NE6-CWM is turned into memorable phrases.

License Plate	Familiar Meaning
NE6-CWM	6 New England states
	Cold Winter Months

Exercise Three

To help you remember the unrelated words in each row, link the words together into a meaningful sentence or two (aim for combining the words in one sentence if possible). It's okay to create wacky and imaginative linkages. After you have created your sentences, read each row of words and the corresponding sentence one at a time. Cover the words and sentence in the row. Then, write down all the words in the row which you can remember.

Words

Ice, Foot, Bee

Sentence

My *foot* that was stung by a *bee* required *icing* because it was so swollen.

a. tire, soap, banana   _____

b. dream, penny, barber, flower   _____

c. computer, envelope, day, cell phone   _____

d. racquet, water, socks, car, blanket   _____

e. bread, milk, peanut butter, chips, soda   _____

Day Six: Acronyms & Acrostics
Skill: First-Letter Linking
Number of Exercises: Two

Items to be remembered can be easily linked together using the first letters of the words to be remembered. This memory technique is called **first-letter linking**. The two most popular variations of first-letter linking are **acronyms**, in which a word is created from the first letters of the items to be remembered, and **acrostics**, in which a sentence is created using words that begin with the first letters of the items to be remembered. Acronyms and acrostics are often taught in schools as study aids.

Example One: Acronyms
Here are three well known examples of acronyms
1. **MADD** – Mothers Against Drunk Driving
2. **NATO** – North American Treaty Organization
3. **ASAP** – As soon as possible

Example Two: Acrostics
Below are two examples of acrostics.
1. **Every good boy does fine** – The lines on a treble note scale: **E, G, B, D, F**
2. **Even Cats Prefer Attention** – The life stages of a butterfly: **egg, caterpillar, pupa, adult**

Exercise One
Study the items and then the acronyms and acrostics in Round One. Then use the acronyms and acrostics to remember the items in Round Two.

Round One
1. Types of blood vessels: capillaries, arteries, veins
   Acronym: CAV

2. Parts of an atom: proton, electron, neutron, shell
   Acronym: PENS

3. The Great Lakes: Huron, Ontario, Michigan, Erie, Superior
   Acronym: HOMES

4. Underwater diving equipment: self-contained underwater breathing apparatus
   Acronym: SCUBA

5. Parts of the eye: cornea, iris, lens, optic nerve, retina
   Acronym: CILOR

6. Earth's oceans: Arctic, Indian, Pacific, Atlantic
   Acronym: AIPA

7. Vitamins important to brain health: B, E, C
   Acronym: BEC

8. Three memory principles: Attention, Imagery, Meaning
   Acronym: AIM

9. The nine planets in our solar system: Mercury, Venus, Earth, Mars, Jupiter, Saturn, Uranus, Neptune, Pluto
   Acrostic: My very energetic mother just served us nine pies.

10. The names of the Beatles: John, Paul, Ringo, George.
    Acrostic: John prefers red grapes

Brainfit

Round Two

1. Name the three types of blood vessels using the acronym CAV.

   _____

   _____

2. Name the four parts of an atom using the acronym PENS.

   _____

   _____

3. Name the Great Lakes using the acronym HOMES.

   _____

   _____

4. Name the underwater diving equipment using the acronym SCUBA.

   _____

   _____

5. Name five parts of the eye using the acronym CILOR.

   _____

   _____

6. Name the oceans of the earth, using the acronym AIPA.

   _____

   _____

7. Name the three vitamins important to brain health, using the acronym BEC.

   _____

   _____

8. Name the three memory principles, using the acronym AIM.

   _____

   _____

9. Name the nine planets in our solar system using the acrostic My Very Energetic Mother Just Served Us Nine Pies.

    _____

    _____

10. Name the four members of the Beatles using the acrostic John Prefers Red Grapes.

    _____

    _____

Exercise Two

Make up acronyms and acrostics to help you remember the information below. Feel free to rearrange the items in a list to make it easier to create a memorable acronym or acrostic.

1. You need to pay the electric, telephone, water, and oil bills. Make up an acrostic to help you remember to pay these bills today.

    _____

    _____

    _____

2 You are going overseas on a business trip. You cannot forget your passport, cell phone, tickets, electrical adaptor, and medication. Make up an acronym or an acrostic to ensure you remember these important items.

    _____

    _____

    _____

3. You are going to the store to pick up some ingredients you need to make your favorite cake recipe. The ingredients are: apples, cinnamon, eggs, walnuts, and brown sugar. Make up an acronym or acrostic you'll remember in the supermarket.

    _____

    _____

    _____

4. Berries high in antioxidants include: blackberries, strawberries, blueberries, and cranberries. Make up an acrostic to help you remember the names of these brain-protecting berries.

_____

_____

_____

5. The five memory skills include Active Observation, Visualization, Verbalization, Linking, and Chunking. Make up an acrostic to help you remember these important memory skills.

_____

_____

_____

6. You have to learn the Seven Deadly Sins for Sunday school. Make up two acrostics or acronyms to help you remember these sins: Pride, Lust, Gluttony, Anger, Envy, Sloth, Greed.

_____

_____

_____

Day Seven: Bite-Size Pieces

Skill: Chunking

Number of Exercises: Two

Chunking lets us break large quantities of information into smaller, more memorable bits that are easier to recall. Based on the research of Harvard psychologist George A. Miller, the average person can hold seven (plus or minus two) items of information in short-term memory.[3] If the information to be remembered is foreign or complex, the chunking limit goes down to three to five items of information.

Example One

We live in a society of numbers and codes. Many important numbers and codes are pre-chunked for us according to George A. Miller's chunking principle. Here are some everyday examples of numbers that have been pre-chunked.

Number Type	Example
Telephone	617-626-3846
Social Security	047-50-6891
Zip Code	02108-1521

Example Two

James, a sales manager, has chunked the things he has to do today into two categories and labeled each category. He then turned the items in each list into acronyms.

Team Communication (SPADE)

Send an e-mail update to boss

Distribute sales guidelines to sales team

Provide feedback to administrative assistant

Attend conference call with regional sales managers

Establish sales goals

Customer Communication (CAW)

Call customer about late product shipment

Approve marketing brochures

Write sales proposal

Example Three

Abdul wants his parents to buy him a dog for his birthday. He has done a lot of research and is particularly fond of the terrier breed. He plans to make his case using the following chunked hierarchy.

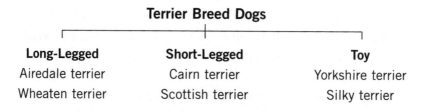

Exercise One:

Group each set of items below into two meaningful chunks of information. Then create a label for each chunk. The first group of items has been chunked and labeled for you. See the end of the chapter for possible solutions.

A. **Items:** basketball, letter, grapefruit, book, quarter, newspaper

Round things	Things you read
basketball	letter
grapefruit	book
quarter	newspaper

B. **Items:** fire, sun, ice, winter, summer, glacier, hot chocolate

C. **Items:** tissue paper, baby, sandpaper, brick, beard, fur

D. **Items:** stamps, faucet, icicle, Post-it Note, glue, popsicle

E. **Items:** coal, snow, tires, tar, vanilla ice cream, polar bear

Exercise Two

Create a list of eight to ten things you have to do in your personal or professional life this week. Chunk the list into two or three meaningful chunks. Then create a label for each chunk.

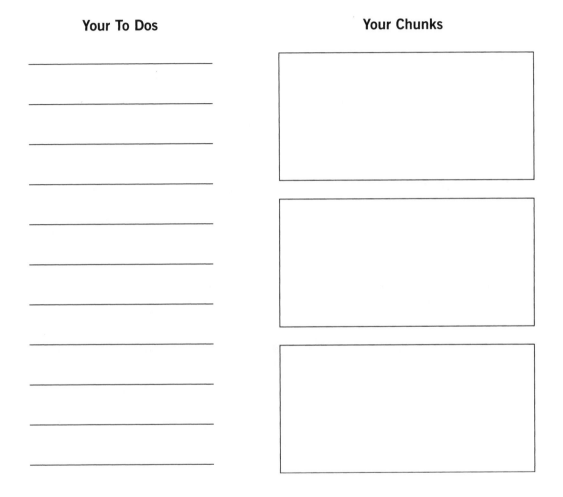

Your To Dos

Your Chunks

*Note: Create common category labels for your To Do lists at home and at the office. Common labels like "outgoing calls," "appointments," "returns," and "pick ups" will be easily memorized and serve as a mental checklist for your daily tasks.

Dr. Brainfit's Advice Column

Dear Dr. Brainfit,

It's pretty common knowledge that stress takes a toll on our physical well-being. What is the effect of stress on memory?

Jose from San Diego

Dear Jose,

Stress is not a friend of memory and mental agility.

Stress and Memory

There are lots of anecdotal stories of memory lapses in stressful situations, like the amateur actor who takes the stage on opening night and suddenly forgets his lines.

A team of researchers, as reported in the journal *Science*, reveal what happens in stressful situations. When people are stressed, they often feel a lack of control. Situations in which we feel a lack of control are found to activate an enzyme in the brain called Protein Kinase C, or PKC. This enzyme was found to impair short-term memory and other functions in the prefrontal cortex of the brain. The prefrontal cortex is the part of the brain associated with executive decision-making. So not only is memory affected, but our decision-making skills are also affected.[4]

Researchers at the University of California, Irvine, working with rats, found that memory interference during stressful situations can be blamed on elevated levels of the hormone cortisol, which is secreted under stress by the human adrenal gland, near the kidneys.[5]

Our body's biochemical responses to stress were once critical protective mechanisms for early man, who needed to be highly alert to changes in his environment. Missing the sound of a twig snapping in the forest could cause danger or even death. Unfortunately, today many people still respond with moderate levels of stress to such everyday triggers as getting stuck in rush hour traffic, taking an exam, or hitting a bad drive off the tee.

Research studies show that most people admit to experiencing stress at least once a day. The cumulative effect of stress in our harried lives is a real and present danger when it comes to mental health and brain health. Most scientists agree that long-term exposure to even low stress levels is likely to accelerate brain aging. So how do we reduce our daily stress levels? Participating in stress-reducing activities such as meditation, yoga, and aerobic exercise can be very beneficial over the long run. For in-the-moment stress, try slow, deep breathing. Close your eyes and envision a calm place. Taking steps to get stress under control is an important part of brain fitness and quality of life.

Solutions

Day Two, Exercise Two: 1. One foot missing a shoe 2. Chair has only three legs 3. Chair back missing a brace 4. Drawing board missing a leg 5. Drawing board missing a brace 5. Boy has one short sleeve and one long sleeve 6. Lamp shines, but is not plugged in 7. Boy wears one long trouser and one short trouser 8. Tree roots have grown into the room 9. Picture frame hangs upside down 10. Waterfall in wall picture is flowing into the room.

Day Two, Exercise Three: Single objects are the cat, the pipe, and the fish lure.

Day Seven, Exercise One: B. hot/cold C. soft/rough D. drip/stick E. black/white

Day Seven, Exercise Two: 1) Items that hold things together: paper clip, bandage, barrette, zipper 2) Items you take when you travel: passport, cell phone, umbrella, suitcase 3) Items found in a bedroom: television, lamp, bed, curtain.

Chapter Four

Remembering Who

"I never forget a face, but in your case
I'll be glad to make an exception."
—GROUCHO MARX

What's in a Name?

Has this ever happened to you? You run into an old acquaintance and begin chatting. You reminisce about the children and your activities together on the PTA board. But try as you will, you cannot remember the person's name. How can you recognize the person's face (I know this person) and recall personal information (I've worked with this person) without being able to surface the person's name?

Scientists have some interesting theories as to why this is so.

All name recognition theories begin with the same basic principle. Recognizing a visual image (a face) is an easier brain process than recalling a fact (a person's name). This explains, in part, why so many memory skills utilize visual cues. According to one popular name recognition theory, the brain stores memories of faces in a different region of the brain than memories of names. So to put a name to a face, the information must be retrieved from two different parts of the brain, and then put together.

Another interesting theory contends that remembering names is a three step process. At each step of the process the brain must recognize or recall a key piece of information in sequence. First, the brain must recognize the person's *facial features*. Second, the brain must link the facial features to *biological data* about the person (such as marital status, occupation, age). Once these two types of information have been accessed, the pathway is clear for the brain to recall the person's *name*. Any breakdown in the process will result in the name not being recalled. This process flow is illustrated below.

Facial Features	**Biological Data**	**Name**
	High School English Teacher Tough Grader Rules Person	Miss Bartley

Sometimes this process happens so quickly we are hardly aware of it. Other times we are painfully aware of the process as we struggle to put a name to a familiar face. Here's an example of how the process might work. Imagine you are walking down Main Street when you see someone coming toward you who is definitely familiar (*facial features recognized*). As he gets closer, you realize it is your son's former high school football coach (*biological data recalled*). But what is his name? "Hey buddy," you say, stalling for time. "How's it going?" you ask, hoping for more biological clues. He starts to tell you about this year's football season. He goes on to mention that his wife, Martha, is home baking cookies for the annual fund-raiser. Suddenly with these additional pieces of information his name clicks into place. His name is Wesley Oaks. You end the conversation by saying, "Well, Wesley, it was great to see you. Give my regards to Martha." In cases like this, where the person is an acquaintance you haven't seen in quite a while, it may take several pieces of biological data to trigger name recall. One of the most famous lines in Shakespeare's *Romeo and Juliet* is when Romeo asks, "What's in a name?" Apparently quite a lot when it comes to recalling names!

Memory Tips for Remembering Names

1. Pay attention to the name when you are introduced.

2 Look, Listen, Repeat (look for a dominant facial feature, listen to the name, repeat the name).

3. Think of ways to link the name to names the brain already knows:
    a. occupations – Singer, Butler, Gardener
    b. famous brands – Campbell, Ford
    c. famous people – Britney, Bush, Monroe
    d. religious figures – Noah, Mary, Moses
    e. animal or thing – Stone, Robin, Bass

4. Create name rhymes (e.g., Heather Feather).

5. Create descriptive adjectives using alliteration (e.g., Daring Darrell).

6. Learn interesting facts about the person, which can serve as memory prompts later.

7. When meeting a new person, pay attention to the circumstances of your meeting, such as where you met and who introduced you. These facts can serve as memory prompts later.

8. Use physical memory aids:
    a. Exchange business or social cards.
    b. Ask the event organizer to use name tags.
    c. Distribute or ask for name rosters in advance of meetings, events, or parties.

9. Don't panic in situations where you know the person, but can't remember the name.
    a. Choose not to be embarrassed . . . everyone forgets names from time to time.
    b. Say, "I know your name, but it seems to be stuck on the tip of my tongue."
    c. Substitute a generic name like buddy, pal, dear, or honey to buy time.
    d. Tell the person you are blanking on his or her name, and ask the person to please provide it again.
    e. Quietly ask someone else to help you with the name.

10. Practice remembering names in everyday situations. Try to remember the names of servers, sales clerks, bank tellers, flight attendants, assistants of business associates, or parents of your children's friends.

What's the Work Out Rationale?

In addition to working on the fundamentals, most athletes also focus on the specific muscle groups needed to excel in their particular sport. To avoid overworking a specific muscle group, athletes often alternate their workout routines, focusing one day on the muscles of the abdomen, and the next on the muscles of the arms or legs. Now that you have mastered the fundamental memory skills of Active Observation, Visualization, Verbalization, Linking, and Chunking, you'll apply these skills to the different "memory muscle groups." When it comes to memory, the five muscle groups include remembering **who, what, how many, when,** and **where**. This week's focus is on remembering *who*.

Let's Work Out!

Welcome to the **Remembering Who** fitness station. As a result of your participation in this week's workout, you'll strengthen your capacity for remembering names. You'll learn how to use select memory skills to enhance your ability to put a name to a face. Using these techniques will help you to store important names in long-term memory, and call them up with greater ease when needed.

Weekly Exercise Planner

The following table lays out the *Brainfit* workout for **Remembering Who**. Each day's workout exercises will be preceded by an Exercise Introduction, which previews the memory skills to be used for the day and provides examples of how the skills will be applied in the exercises.

Day	Exercise Name	Skill	Pages
Day One	Picture This	Visualization Linking	83–84
Day Two	Image Building	Verbalization Visualization Linking	85–87
Day Three	Spotting Striking Features	Visualization Active Observation Linking	88–90
Day Four	Potato Head Game	Active Observation Linking	91–92
Day Five	Name Exposure	Verbalization Visualization	93–97
Day Six	Sound Play	Verbalization	98–99
Day Seven	Who's on the Team?	First-Letter Linking	100–101

Day One: Picture This

Skills: Visualization and Linking
Number of Exercises: One

Some names have built-in imagery, which we can use to secure a name in memory. Using name imagery is a fun and easy way to boost name recognition and recall.

Example One

Your new duplicate bridge partner is Rose Weiner. Remembering names has never been your strong suit, and as you've gotten older, remembering them has become a little more challenging. Applying the visualization memory skill, you recognize immediately that Rose Weiner is a name with built-in imagery. *Rose* is both a flower and a color which you can see in your mind's eye. *Weiner* is slang for hot dog. In your mind you conjure up the picture of an undercooked, rose-colored hot dog. To link the image to the name, you picture Rose Weiner eating an undercooked, rose-colored hot dog at the annual bridge luncheon.

Example Two

Your new customer service representative is named Barbara Singer. Using the built-in imagery in the name, you picture a singing Barbie doll dressed in a classy office outfit talking on a cell phone.

Exercise One

Below is a list of twelve names. Each name has built-in imagery. Your task is to find a concrete image associated with each name. The first one is done for you. After you've created images for all of the names, cover Column A. Then, "read" the images you created, one at a time, in Column B. See how many names you can remember from the images you created. Write the names you can remember in Column C.

A. Name	B. Concrete Image	C. Name
1. *Angela Basso*	*A bass fish with an angel riding on its back.*	
2. Julie Paige	_____	_____

A. Name	B. Concrete Image	C. Name
3. Sandy Tiffany	_____	_____
4. Red Armstrong	_____	_____
5. Harry Knott	_____	_____
6. Noah Watercress	_____	_____
7. Fulbright Mellin	_____	_____
8. Gracie Birch	_____	_____
9. Melanie Greene	_____	_____
10. Art Malis	_____	_____
11. Carmen Crane	_____	_____
12. Lacy Doile	_____	_____

Day Two: Image Building

Skills: Verbalization, Visualization, and Linking
Number of Exercises: Two

Not all names have built-in imagery, but many names have image-building potential. Playing with the sounds in a name will often conjure up images that were not immediately apparent. Here is a process you can use to tap the image potential in almost any name.

1. Break the name into syllables (override grammar rules to create meaningful sounds and images).
2. Sound out the syllables, looking for words or sounds that trigger images.
3. Create vivid mental images.
4. Link the images and the name together in a colorful mental picture.

Example One

You've been referred to a new hair stylist named Jimmy Sorrento. You've been told he is very temperamental and prefers to be called his full name. To better remember his name, you use the process described above. *Sorrento,* if broken down into syllables (sorr-en-to), might conjure up the image of a sore toe. Pumping up the image to make it more vivid, you might visualize a festering sore on a hairy big toe. To weave in the first name, *Jimmy,* you picture chocolate "jimmies" (sprinkles) embedded in the sore. Pretty gross, but definitely memorable!

Example Two

Last week you were introduced to the new president of the League of Women Voters. Her name is Carole Kane. Carole Kane, of course, sounds like Candy Cane. To ensure you remember her name at your next league meeting, you picture Carole sucking on a red, white, and blue striped candy cane, which she occasionally uses as a gavel on the speaking podium.

Example Three

Some names refuse to convert easily into images despite our best efforts. In these situations, you will need to get really creative. Use humor, exaggeration, and creative leaps of faith to transform these names into images. For example:

Name	Syllables	Sounds Like	Concrete Image
Claudia	Claud-dia	Clawed diva	An opera star(diva)being clawed by her white angora cat
Moura	Mour-a	Morose	A morose woman singing the blues
Mr. Zimmerman	Zimmer-man	Simmer-man	A man stirring a pot of Campbell's soup

Exercise One

Your goal is to come up with a concrete image, which will help you remember each of the names listed in Column A. The names have been converted into syllables for you in Column B. Your job is to complete Columns C and D. After you have finished the exercise, cover Columns A through C. See how many names you can recall using the concrete images you created in Column D. Write the names you can remember on a piece of scrap paper. See the end of the chapter for possible responses to column D.

A Name	B Syllables	C Sounds Like	D Concrete Image
Gediman	*Ged-i-man*	*Get a man*	*A man who's been lassoed*
1. Barney	Bar- ney	_____	_____
2. Robinsky	Robin-sky	_____	_____
3. Morello	Mor-ello	_____	_____
4. Greenberg	Green-berg	_____	_____
5. Petzy	Pet-zy	_____	_____

A	B	C	D
Name	Syllables	Sounds Like	Concrete Image
6. Grayham	Gray-ham	_____	_____
7. Toomey	Too-mey	_____	_____
8. Corliss	Cor-liss	_____	_____
9. Abisso	A-bis-so	_____	_____
10. Ramiro	Ra-mir-o	_____	_____

Exercise Two

In the mix and match exercise below, connect each name with its appropriate image. Then check your responses against the answer key at the end of the chapter.

Name	Image
1. Burdeau	a. a beautiful day garden filled with morning glories
2. Nearworny	b. a "no sir" sign on a women's restroom
3. Struhl	c. a crystal chandelier handing in a foyer
4. Primmer	d. an army commander leading the charge
5. Serno	e. a vast orchestra of con men playing cellos
6. Desjardin	f. a charlatan selling useless potions from a tent
7. Accomando	g. a prim and proper librarian
8. Christoforo	h. a piece of warm, baked strudel
9. Vasconcellos	i. an ear filled with worms
10. Charlebois	j. a doe with a bird on its back

Day Three: Spotting Striking Features

Skills: Visualization, Active Observation, Linking
Number of Exercises: Two

As you know, visual images produce powerful memory hooks. Just as people's personalities are unique, so are their facial features. Linking a prominent facial feature to a person's name is a proven memory technique for improving name recall.

When you are introduced to someone, pay attention to his prominent or striking facial features. Does she have ears as big as megaphones or as small as seashells? Is his nose bulbous or aquiline? Are her lips thick and fleshy, or narrow and thin? Link the dominant facial feature with the person.

Example One

Political cartoonists love to link famous people with their prominent facial features. President George W. Bush is often pictured with oversized ears. President Bill Clinton was often pictured with a bulbous nose.

Example Two

Mark remembers people by making up nicknames that incorporate a person's striking facial feature. He picks striking features that begin with the same letter as the person's name. Here are some examples of nicknames he uses to remember people's names.

Name	Feature	Nickname
John	large mouth	Johnny Jaw
Lucy	long eyelashes	Lucy Lashes

Exercise One

Below is a list of names of famous people. See if you can call to mind a striking facial feature associated with each name. If you do not recognize a name, look it up on the Internet, or ask a friend to prompt your memory. The first one is done for you. See the end of the chapter for a list of possible responses.

Name	**Striking Facial Feature**
1. Chelsea Clinton	*Curly hair*
2. Michael Jackson	_____
3. Ross Perot	_____
4. Angelina Jolie	_____
5. Adolph Hitler	_____
6. Paul Newman	_____
7. Barbra Streisand	_____
8. John Travolta	_____
9. Jay Leno	_____
10. Arnold Schwarzenegger	_____
11. Elton John	_____
12. Julia Roberts	_____

Exercise Two [1]

Round One

Study each pair of faces below for five seconds. Identify a dominant or striking feature on the faces of each pair. In round two, you will use these features to remember which faces were paired. After you have studied the paired faces, turn the page and see how many correct matches you can make. *Repeat* the entire exercise *three* times.

Round Two

Match up the numbers with the appropriate letters to recreate the paired faces.

1. _____   4. _____
2. _____   5. _____
3. _____   6. _____

The norms for this exercise are:

First Effort: Two correct matches for individuals aged 60 to 70 years old; three correct matches for individuals aged 18 to 23 years old.

Second Effort: Two correct for older individuals; four correct for younger individuals.

Third Effort: Three correct for older individuals; five correct for younger individuals.

Day Four: Potato Head Game

Skills: Active Observation and Linking
Number of Exercises: Two

Do you remember the child's toy called Mr. Potato Head? It consisted of a blank head shaped like a potato, which came with assorted plastic facial features that you could paste or push onto the potato head to create different people. In the next exercise, you'll combine three memory skills to create your own memorable Potato Head. Since you will be working with multiple skills, the process may feel a little cumbersome at first. With time, however, this approach can become quite natural and fun. Here's how it works:

1. Identify a striking facial feature.
2. Look for an image built into the name.
3. Mentally paste the "name image" onto the striking feature.

Example

The new manager at your bank branch is named Ms. Isabelle. You own a small business and have a lot of interaction with the bank manager, so you want to remember her name. Ms. Isabelle has beautiful red hair, a striking feature. Her name converts easily to the image of a *bell*. To remember Ms. Isabelle's name visualize tiny silver bells woven into her beautiful red hair.

Exercise One

Now it's your turn to play the Potato Head Game. This is a multiskill application exercise, so the degree of difficulty is high. Be patient and have fun with it. Remember, the more challenging the exercise, the more brain activity you're stimulating! The first one is done for you. Your task is to fill in Column B (find an image associated with the name) and Column D (mentally paste the image on the striking feature). If you are artistically inclined, instead of using words, feel free to draw a picture of your "potato head" on a separate piece of paper. Check for possible solutions to column D at the end of the chapter.

A	B	C	D
Name	**Image**	**Striking Feature**	**The Potato Head**
Barbette	*Barrette*	*pony tail*	*A rhinestone barrette holding a pony tail*
Horne	_____	Grizzly beard	_____
Mayberry	_____	Ruddy cheeks	_____
Sorrow	_____	Big blue eyes	_____
Woods	_____	Toothy smile	_____
Seinfeld	_____	Wide forehead	_____

Exercise Two

In this exercise you will create names that capitalize on a prominent feature. First, examine each of the five faces below and circle one striking feature on each face. Then make up a first or last name for each face that builds on the striking feature you circled. For example, if the striking feature you circled is *glasses*, you might give the person the last name of *Glassman*.

Day Five: Name Exposure
Skills: Verbalization and Visualization
Number of Exercises: Three

The more exposure we have to a name, the more likely we are to remember it. That's why it is fairly easy to recall the names of famous and infamous people who are in the news regularly, be they politicians, movie stars, or criminals. Conversely, when we are introduced to someone only once, or run into that person infrequently, the reduced name exposure makes name retrieval more challenging. One way to remember names better is simply to hear the name repeated more often.

Verbalization
- Repeat the name out loud.
- Really listen as the name is used by others.

Visualization
- See the name as it is written.

Example One

Mark is preparing for an international business seminar he will soon be facilitating. When working with international populations, Mark always asks for the participant roster in advance. Out of respect for other cultures, he wants to make sure he can pronounce each of the names on the list correctly. As he scans the roster, there is one name he knows will give him trouble. It is the Indian name, Anuradha Baskhshi. To be sure he will be able to pronounce and remember the name, he rehearses it several times out loud until he is comfortable with the sounds and flow of the name.

Example Two

Amanda is a tour guide at the United Nations. She is always meeting new people and must pick up names quickly. Each time she meets a new person she uses a simple three-step technique that combines verbalization with visualization. First, she mentally repeats the name three times. Second, she visualizes the name written on the person's forehead in a bold primary color. Third, she imagines herself writing the name using a crayon of the same bold color.

Example Three

When meeting a person for the first time, a proven way to boost name exposure is to repeat the person's name as many times as possible in the initial conversation. Here's a process you can use for conversational name repetition, followed by an example. It may feel a little awkward at first, but over time it can become quite natural.

1. **Repeat the Name**

   "Anne Sullivan, I want to welcome you to our book club."

2. **Comment on the Name**

   "Is Anne spelled with or without an *e* at the end?"

3. **Insert the Name in Conversation**

   "So, Anne, what did you think of our book selection?"

4. **End with the Person's Name**

   "It was nice meeting you, Anne Sullivan, and I hope we'll see you at our book club next month."

Exercise One

In this exercise, you will challenge your brain to recall the names of famous people with high name exposure. Brainstorm as many names as you can for each category, or challenge your friends to a name trivia contest. Allow one minute per name category. See who can come up with the greatest number of names in one minute.

1. Comedians

   _____

   _____

   _____

2. Criminals

   _____

   _____

   _____

3. Movie stars

_____

_____

_____

4. Writers

_____

_____

_____

5. Athletes

_____

_____

_____

6. Newscasters

_____

_____

_____

7. Politicians

_____

_____

_____

8. Musicians

_____

_____

_____

9. Painters

_____

_____

_____

10. Scientists

_____

_____

_____

11. Golfers

_____

_____

_____

12. Singers

_____

_____

_____

13. Presidents of the twentieth century

_____

_____

_____

14. Talk show hosts

_____

_____

_____

How did you do? Some categories were probably easier than others depending on your own personal interest areas.

Exercise Two

Practice using conversational name repetition in the two scenarios below. The process for name repetition is outlined for you. Your job is to fill in the conversation at each step in the process. Speak each step in the process out loud.

Scenario 1: You are being introduced to your spouse's boss at the holiday party. Your spouse works in the marketing department at XYZ Corporation. The boss's name is Sam Pierson.

1. Repeat the name
2. Comment on the name
3. Use the name in conversation
4. End with the person's name

Scenario 2: Think of a real-world situation in which you recently met someone new. Use the name repetition process to boost your exposure to this new name.

1. Repeat the name
2. Comment on the name
3. Use the name in conversation
4. End with the name

How did you do? The repetition skill model is helpful because it ensures that you actively pay attention to the person's name. Sometimes just paying real attention can make all the difference in the world between a name remembered and a name forgotten.

Day Six: Sound Play

Skills: Verbalization
Number of Exercises: Two

Example One

Rhymes and alliteration are forms of verbalization that help us store and recall names better. Below are some examples of **name rhymes** and **name alliteration** that create strong memory hooks. When using name alliteration, you make up a descriptive adjective that begins with the same first letter of the person's first and/or last name. It is helpful if the adjective correlates to some memorable aspect of the person's physical features or personality. Here are some examples of name rhyming and name alliteration.

Name	Rhyme	Alliteration
Dan	Dan the Man	Dapper Dan
Mary Ellen	Mary Ellen Watermelon	Merry Mary
Jack	Jack the Running Back	Jumping Jack
Louie	Screwy Louie	Loony Louie
Dennis	Dennis the Menace	Daring Dennis
Nancy	Antsy Nancy	Nervous Nancy

Exercise One

For each of the first names listed below, create a name rhyme or come up with a descriptive adjective using alliteration.

Name	Rhyme	Alliteration
1. Heather	_____	_____
	_____	_____
2. Tim	_____	_____
	_____	_____

Name	Rhyme	Alliteration
3. Mark	_____	_____
	_____	_____
4. Amanda	_____	_____
	_____	_____
5. Molly	_____	_____
	_____	_____
6. Max	_____	_____
	_____	_____

Exercise Two

Repeat the exercise above for three real acquaintances of yours. Pick individuals whose names you've recently learned and want to make sure to remember. Or choose names you sometimes blank on.

Name	Rhyme	Alliteration
1. _____	_____	_____
	_____	_____
2. _____	_____	_____
	_____	_____
3. _____	_____	_____
	_____	_____

Day Seven: Who's on the Team?

Skills: First-Letter Linking
Number of Exercises: Three

When you have to remember a group of names, first-letter linking can be a most effective memory tool. As you'll recall, the two most common forms of first-letter linking are acronyms and acrostics. In each of the exercises below, devise an acronym or an acrostic to help you remember the group of names. Feel free to rearrange the order of the names to make it easier to create your acronyms and acrostics.

Acronyms

Create or make up a new word using the first letters of the names to be remembered: *Mary, Anthony, Denise = MAD*

Acrostics

Create a sentence using words with the first letters of the names to be remembered: *Victor, Inez, Martha = Venus Invades Mars*

Example

Suppose you are responsible for introducing the new sales team at an upcoming business function. The people on the team are: Mary, Arthur, Donald, Elizabeth, Gregory, and Gail. While you know these people's names, you get nervous when speaking publicly. So you decide to devise an acronym that will serve as a memory prompt. Using the first letters of each name, you come up with two acronyms, MAD EGG.

Exercise One

You have been named as the chairperson of the school fund-raiser. The parents who have volunteered to be on your committee are Jenny, Ellen, Linda, Lionel, and Evan. Create an acronym or an acrostic to serve as a memory prompt.

Exercise Two

You enjoy acting in community theater. The new cast members for the fall production are Julia, Louise, Ned, Arthur, and Harriet. Devise an acronym or an acrostic to help you remember the cast members' names.

_____

_____

Exercise Three

Think of a real group of which you are a member (for example, family, friends, clubs, organizations, business). Write down the first names of the group members. Then create an acronym or acrostic that would help you remember the names of the people in your group.

_____

_____

Dr. Brainfit's Advice Column

Dear Dr. Brainfit,

My roommate and I are having a disagreement about the best approach to studying for exams. Is it better to sleep the night before a big exam or pull an all-nighter?

Rosa from NYC

Dear Rosa,

How you study best is an individual choice For example, some people can only study with background noise, while others find this distracting. When it comes to sleeping or cramming before that big exam, here is what the experts have to say.

Sleep on It

Staying up late to cram for an exam may be counterproductive when it comes to memory and performance. Recent studies demonstrate that a good night's sleep is required for memory consolidation. Memory consolidation is the process by which experience or training is transformed into improvements in performance.

There are two basic types of sleep: slow wave sleep (deep slumber) and REM sleep (rapid eye movement). Slow wave sleep, which makes up the majority of the sleep cycle, precedes REM sleep. In a research paper by Steffen Gais of Germany, it was found that slow wave sleep alone was sufficient for task learning, but that both types of sleep were required for maximal increase in performance. According to John Spiro, in an accompanying editorial, "the average person requires eight hours of sleep per night . . . but many otherwise healthy people continually deprive themselves of adequate sleep with consequences that include fatigue, poor decision-making and increased risk of accidents." So when people tell you to "sleep on it" before making an important decision or taking an exam, they are giving you sound advice.[5]

Solutions

Day Two, Exercise One (possible responses column D): 1. knee with a stick attached 2. robin on skis 3. Jell-O pouring into a bowl 4. green hamburger 5. pet zebra 6. gray ham 7. twins 8. apple without a core 9. rain on windowsill 10. a bee sewing 11. men in blue socks 12. rearview mirror

Day Two, Exercise Two (possible responses): 1j, 2i, 3h, 4g, 5b, 6a, 7d, 8c, 9e, 10f

Day Three, Exercise One (possible responses): 1. curly hair 2. diminutive nose 3. big ears 4. big, full lips 5. brush moustache 6. blue eyes 7. prominent nose 8. cleft chin 9. long chin 10. square face 11. wacky glasses 12. radiant smile

Day Four, Exercise One (possible responses): 1. A French horn resting on a thick, grizzly beard; 2. Ruddy cheeks stained with red berries; 3. Weepy blue eyes; 4. A smile with toothpicks instead of teeth; 5. A bright red felt sign on a shiny white forehead.

Chapter Five

Remembering What

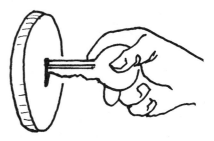

*"It is not good enough for things to be planned—
they still have to be done; for intention to become
reality, energy has to be launched into operation."*
—Pir Viayat Inayat Khan

Turning Intentions into Actions

A primary brain function, which distinguishes humans from other mammals, is the ability to form an intention and then act on that intention at a future time. The mental capacity to remember to do something in the future is called **prospective memory**. It is also one of the least understood and most challenging of memory functions. Prospective memory is a hot, new field of study, drawing the attention of many top neuropyschologists.

On an everyday basis, our intentions make up the better part of our waking hours. When we get up in the morning one of our first thoughts is, "What do I have to do today?" Before we go to bed we worry, "Did I do everything I was supposed to do today?" We fill up Post-it Notes, calendars, and electronic gadgets with our intentions, hoping that these devices will help us to turn our intentions into actions.

There are three factors that make remembering to take future actions challenging. The first challenge is the *time delay factor*. If I think of it now, will I remember to do it later? The second challenge is *ongoing distractions*. Between now and then, there are many other priorities and interruptions that will occupy my attention. The third challenge is a *lack of future retrieval cues*. What memory cues will prompt me to take action at a future date? Even the simplest of intentions can fall prey to these three challenges. Take the following example. You wake up in the morning and notice an overdue library book on your night table. You form an intention to return the book to the library this afternoon when you go grocery shopping. During the morning you read the paper, do the laundry, pay bills, return phone calls, work out on the treadmill, shower, and blow-dry your hair. After lunch, you make up your grocery list and head out to the supermarket. When you get home, you put away the groceries and prepare an after-school snack for the kids. That evening when you get into bed you notice the overdue library book gathering dust on your night table. Any surprises here?

Creating Retrieval Cues for Future Actions

Ever heard of the absentminded professor? You may be a brilliant physicist who can remember hundreds of equations, but this is no guarantee that you will remember to pick up milk on the way home or keep your dentist appointment. Researchers agree that one key to remembering our future actions is to build retrieval cues right into our intentions. These retrieval cues can be tied to a person, place, event, or time frame. For instance, you might form an intention this way: *when I see Tom (person) at work (place) in our Monday morning meeting (place and time), I'll ask him for the phone number of his cardiologist.*

Memory Tips for Remembering What

1. Leave environmental prompts in conspicuous and odd places to signal there is some action you must take. For example, place a return package on top of your car, leave the blinds down in your office.

2. Alter your physical appearance to signal that an action needs to be taken. Wear your watch on the opposite wrist.
3. Place Post-it Notes strategically around the house.
4. Make a To Do list and check it morning, noon, and night. Keep a copy in your car.
5. Try using electronic devices with built-in retrieval cues, like phones with memory functions, computer calendars, and electronic organizers.
6. Turn your To Do list into pictures or symbols that have visual memory impact.
7. Use direct deposit and direct bill-paying services available through your bank to ensure that your checks are deposited promptly and that important bills are paid on time.
8. To overcome absentmindedness related to your immediate intentions:

Stop

Focus

Do it now

What's the Workout Rationale?

There is nothing more frustrating than finding that something important you meant to do has fallen through the cracks. After forgetting names, this type of memory error is the next most common memory complaint. The lament sounds something like this, "I can't believe I forgot to . . ." When actions we intend to take don't happen because we forget, it creates unnecessary stress and unwanted feelings of incompetence.

Let's Work Out!

Welcome to the **Remembering What** fitness station. As a result of your participation in this week's workout, you'll get better at following through on your intended actions. You'll learn how to create external environmental cues and internal memory cues for remembering what you need to do. As you work out, you'll continue to sharpen your memory by using the fundamental memory skills of Active Observation, Linking, Visualization, Verbalization, and Chunking.

Weekly Exercise Planner

The following table lays out the *Brainfit* workout for **Remembering What.** Each day's workout exercises will be preceded by an Exercise Introduction. The Exercise Introduction previews the memory skills to be used for the day and provides examples of how the skills will be applied in the exercises.

Day	Exercise Name	Skill	Pages
Day One	Immediate Intentions	Verbalization Visualization	107–111
Day Two	Environmental Prompts	Active Observation Visualization	112–113
Day Three	Loci Method	Linking Visualization	114–117
Day Four	Colorful Categories	Chunking Visualization	118–122
Day Five	Powerful Pairs	Linking Visualization	123–125
Day Six	Storytelling	Verbalization Visualization Linking	126–127
Day Seven	Hot Potato	Linking	128–129

Day One: Immediate Intentions

Skills: Verbalization and Visualization
Number of Exercises: Three

Most people have heard of a To Do list. These lists contain the things we need to get done today or this week. They include items like making important phone calls, running errands, and completing important tasks or chores. But how many of you have heard of a Didn't Do list? See if any of these *didn't dos* have a familiar ring to them.

Honey, you left the house unlocked.
Dear, you didn't close the garage door and the raccoon got into the trash.
Bob, didn't you say you were sending me an e-mail right away?
Mom, I thought you said you were going to call me right back.

These memory *faux pas* are examples of how easy it is to forget our immediate intentions. We intend to do something in the moment and then, much to our own amazement, we simply forget to take action. The single biggest culprit involved in forgetting to take action in the moment is a lack of attention. We unwittingly allow some interference to draw us away from our intended action. Two helpful guidelines for overcoming this type of memory problem are 1) Do it now and 2) Do one thing at a time. In addition, the memory skills of verbalization and visualization can help boost in-the-moment focus. Use verbal self-instruction to reinforce your immediate intention. Speak, rhyme, or sing your purpose. Create a strong visual image that will serve as a prompt for your intended action.

Example One

Jane frequently forgets to lock the door when she leaves the house. While this is not of great concern to her, it does upset her spouse. She decides to use the following rhyme, on a regular basis, to reinforce her intention to lock the door.

"I am locking the door as I go out,
If I forget my spouse will shout."

Example Two

John has been very stressed at work lately, and not surprisingly he has become more absentminded at work and at home. Just yesterday, he found himself standing in the middle of the office mailroom with no recollection of what he had come to do. Last night he headed into the kitchen with a purpose in mind, but he was distracted by the dog barking at the back door. He let the dog out and returned to the kitchen, only to forget his original purpose. To remedy this situation, John turns to *verbal self-instruction*. He hopes this will combat his temporary bout of absentmindedness. Here are a few examples of the verbal self-instruction he uses to stay focused and sane.

"I am going into the kitchen to get a pair of scissors."
"I am going to the mailroom to see if the FedEx package has arrived."
"I am logging off the Internet so I don't tie up the telephone line."

Example Three

Mornings at the Delaney house are a zoo. Everyone is in a rush. Mr. Delaney is trying to get out the door before 7:00, so he will beat the rush hour traffic. The kids need to get to the bus stop on time. If they miss the bus it throws off everyone's schedule. Mrs. Delaney needs to get sandwiches in the kids' lunch boxes and take the dog out before going to work. The one thing Mrs. Delaney always seems to forget is taking the meat out of the freezer so it will be defrosted in time for dinner. When she forgets, which is often, the family ends up eating cereal or scrambled eggs for dinner. This makes her feel very guilty and ruins everyone's evening.

In desperation, Mrs. Delaney turns to *visualization* to imprint in her mind the action of defrosting the meat before leaving the house. First she creates a vivid image of a red and bloody piece of meat that is in the process of defrosting. Then she mentally pastes the image on the garage door. She sees the meat hanging from the door on a butcher's meat hook. To further boost her memory and sharpen the image, she looks for an environmental prompt to attach to the door. She finds a red ribbon that she coils around the door knob. Mrs. Delaney is hopeful that forgetting to defrost the meat is a thing of the past.

Exercise One

Make up a simple rhyme that will reinforce your intention to take the following immediate actions. The first one is done for you. Your task is to fill in the second line of each remaining rhyme.

Rhyme Example

I am going to the bedroom to get my sweater.

If I get my sweater, I'll feel better.

Rhyme One

I am signing off the Internet for the night.

_____

Rhyme Two

I'm shutting off the coffeepot.

_____

Rhyme Three

I'm putting my ring on the kitchen shelf.

_____

Rhyme Four

I am taking my pill.

_____

Rhyme Five

I am going upstairs to check my e-mail.

_____

Exercise Two

Create a vivid mental image that will reinforce the need to take the following immediate actions. The first one is done for you.

Action	Image
Turn off the stove.	*Every time you use the stove, visualize the color red. See your hand in a bright red kitchen mitt, turning off a glowing red burner knob.*

Shut the open fireplace flue. _____

Turn on the alarm system as
you leave the house. _____

Take your cell phone with
you as you leave the car. _____

Lock the office safe. _____

Put your credit card back
in your wallet. _____

Exercise Three

Now let's apply memory skills to your own in-the-moment chores. Follow the five steps below to make remembering immediate intentions part of your everyday habit.

Step One: List Immediate Intentions

Create a list of immediate intentions that you sometimes forget to do. Your list should contain items you tend to "double check," as well as items that prompt you to ask, "Did I do that?" Below is a sample list of immediate intentions people sometimes forget.

Sample List   **My List**

Turn off the stove   _____

Turn off the iron   _____

Lock the door   _____

Turn on the alarm   _____

Leave water for the dog/cat   _____

Turn off the outside lights   _____

Take your daily vitamins and medicines   _____

Sample List	My List
Put your glasses back in the case	_____
Put the TV remote away	_____
Return the cordless phone to the charger unit	_____
Put your credit card back in your wallet	_____
Put the gas cap back on the gas tank	_____

Step Two: Use verbal self-instruction

As you go through your normal day, use *verbal self-instruction* for each item on your list. Say what you are doing out loud as you do it. For example you might say, "I am putting my credit card back in my wallet." Stating out loud what you are doing is an excellent way to boost in-the-moment focus and combat absentmindedness. If you are uncomfortable speaking out loud then say the action silently in your mind. Do not try to memorize the list or carry it with you. At the end of the day, check off all the items on your list for which you successfully used verbal self-instruction. Star the items you did not need to double check as a result of using verbal self-instruction.

Step Three: Use Visualization

Tomorrow add *visualization* to your verbal self-instruction: actually see yourself taking the immediate action. Imagine your mind is a camera. Take a color snapshot of your in-the-moment action. For instance, see your hand putting the red sales receipt in the third compartment of your brown wallet. At the end of the day, check off those items on your list for which you successfully used visualization and verbal self-instruction. Star the items you did not need to double check as a result of your skill use.

Step Four: Repeat the Process

Repeat Steps One through Three for one full week. At the end of the week, ask yourself "Is this helping?" If the answer is *yes,* make verbal self-instruction and visualization part of your daily habit.

Day Two: Environmental Prompts

Skills: Active Observation and Visualization
Number of Exercises: Three

Remembering to do something in the future requires a trigger. Triggers can be internal memory cues, external memory aids (like a To Do list, calendar, or Palm Pilot) and environmental prompts. Environmental prompts are objects, events, people, and places that when encountered will remind you to take action. For example, breakfast is the event that reminds you to take your vitamins. To create a powerful environmental prompt, you first select your prompt. Look for people, places, events, and objects that will catch your attention. Then you make the prompt more memorable by using the memory skill of visualization. Use vivid images, real and imagined, to make environmental prompts more memorable.

Example One

Samantha wants to remember to get the phone number of the local veterinarian from her friend, Bob. Samantha and Bob are going to be at the Cub Scout picnic on Saturday. Samantha's environmental prompts are Bob (person), place (picnic), and date (Saturday). She makes her environmental prompt more memorable by visualizing Bob in the friendly body of her Saint Bernard barking a hello in his strong, bass voice.

Example Two

Trish needs to stop off at the bank to get cash. The bank is located on Beacon Street. She passes Beacon Street to and from work daily. She uses Beacon Street as her environmental prompt. She pumps up the image by visualizing a flashing green-and-red beacon on top of the street sign. In her mind she associates the color green with *cash* and the color red with *stop*.

Example Three

Katrina leaves all of her vitamins and medicines on the kitchen table so she will remember to take them daily. While this works as an environmental prompt, it's messy and embarrassing when people come to visit. Katrina knows she still needs a prompt, but she wants to find something less visible. So she puts her vitamins and medicines away in the cabinet above the kitchen sink. She purchases a sun-catcher that dangles from a nylon thread. She secures the nylon thread to the inside of the cabinet so that the sun-catcher catches the light from the kitchen window. Now every time she goes to the sink, which is several times a day, she sees the sun-catcher sparkling. In her mind she associates the sparkling sun-catcher with the good health she will enjoy when she takes her vitamins and medicines.

Exercise One

Listed below are some routine items that appear on many people's errand lists. For each errand on the list, create an environmental prompt that will remind you to take action. Be creative! The more odd or unusual the environmental prompt, the more likely it will catch your attention.

Errands	Environmental Prompt
Bring back overdue library books	Put your library card on your car visor.
Pick up fish for dinner	
Get stamps at post office	
Return video/DVD	
Make dentist appointment	
Refill medicine prescription	
Pay overdue electric bill	
Pick up birthday card for Dad	

Exercise Two

Create a living memory board for your home or office. Hang the board (poster board, cork board, magnetic board, etc.) in a place you pass by many times a day (kitchen, office cubicle wall, back door, etc.). Buy or create symbols that stand for common tasks or errands. Each day place the symbols for the day's tasks or errands on the board. At the end of the day, when the tasks and errands have been completed, remove the symbols. Physically interacting with your memory board on a daily basis is fun and a sure way to prevent things from slipping through the cracks. Have a contest with your family or work team to see who can come up with the most creative memory board.

Day Three: Loci Method
Skills: Linking and Visualization
Number of Exercises: Two

The *internal* memory equivalent of the environmental prompt is the **Loci method**. It is the oldest known mnemonic strategy, as it was used by the Greeks around 500 B.C. According to Cicero, the method was developed by a poet named Simonides of Ceos after a tragic event. A building in which Simonides was speaking collapsed during a dinner party. Simonides, the only survivor, was able to remember the names of the dead by visualizing where they were sitting at the table. By remembering their *location* at the dinner party, he was able to remember their names. He concluded that linking an item to be remembered with a specific location could improve a person's memory.

The method is still very popular today with many memory experts. Here is how it works. Pick an architectural structure. This could be your house or a particular room in your house. Then mentally move through the structure in a logical order. Suppose you are using your house as your structure. You might start at your front door, then mentally move from the dining room, to the kitchen, to the living room, and up the stairs to the bedrooms. Place each item to be remembered in a different room of the house, or on a different physical object within a single room. Create vivid and wacky images that link each item to be remembered with its physical location in the house or room. When you want to remember the items, mentally walk back through your memory house (or room) and recall the images you attached to each location. If you prefer, you can use locations on your body (e.g. head, arm, leg), instead of locations in your house. Attach items to be remembered to physical locations on your body. Create a vivid wacky image that connects the item to be remembered to its physical location on your body.

Example One
Roberto makes a grocery list of four items he needs at the supermarket: eggs, bread, salad vegetables, and chicken. First he chooses his *Loci* location, which is his living room. Then he selects five objects in his living room, one for each of the items on his grocery list. On the next page is the *Loci* system he creates. When he gets to the supermarket he will mentally walk past each object in his living room and recall the image he has attached to it. Since he is just learning the *Loci* method, he'll take his grocery list with him as backup.

Item	Object	Image
Eggs	Coffee Table	Picture multi-colored eggs displayed on the coffee table like mini-sculptures. Each egg has its own golden display stand with the artist's name engraved.
Bread	Fireplace	Picture a baker with a big white hat and white flour on his rosy cheeks, pulling burnt bread out of a raging fire.
Salad Vegetables	Oriental Rug	Picture Peter Rabbit scratching at your oriental rug with a garden hoe. He is carving rows in the carpet, so he can plant vegetables in the spring.
Chicken	Sofa	Picture a scruffy, yellow chicken pecking at your sofa, creating little holes in the leather fabric.

Example Two

Donna, who is terrified of speaking publicly, is attending classes in public speaking sponsored by her company. Next week she has to give a five-minute speech about unique aspects of her upbringing without using notes. She plans to use the *Loci* method to ensure she remembers all her key points. She chooses to attach the key points of her speech to specific parts of her body. She links each key point to its respective body part using fanciful images. Here is her *Loci* speech outline.

Key Point	Body Part	Image
Grew up in Kansas	Head	The letter "K" sitting on her head
Lived on a farm	Shoulders	A red silo balanced on her shoulders
Was homeschooled until age ten	Arms	Her arms loaded with schoolbooks
Had nine brothers and sisters	Hips	Baby brothers and sisters riding on her hips
Won the county spelling bee	Feet	A bee resting on her shoe

As she practices her speech, she mentally moves from one body part to the next in a logical order starting with her head and ending with her feet. During her speech she follows the same approach.

Exercise One

Select a store in which you need to buy several key items this week. Pick a store in which you regularly shop. Make a list of five key items you need to purchase at the store. Prior to going shopping, review the list and create your own memory house to help you remember the items on the list. Put the list in the glove compartment of your car. As you shop, use your memory house to help you remember the items you need to buy. See if you can get through your shopping, without running back to your car to look at the list. If you forget an item, it is because the image you created is not memorable enough. Use the framework below to build your memory house. An example has been provided to get you started. While this may not be an approach you would choose to use on a regular basis, it is a great memory and mental agility exercise to go through at least once.

Item	Room	Object	Image
Bananas	*Office*	*Printer*	*Visualize banana peels rolling through the printer instead of computer paper.*
1. _____	_____	_____	_____
			_____
2. _____	_____	_____	_____
			_____
3. _____	_____	_____	_____
			_____
4. _____	_____	_____	_____
			_____
5. _____	_____	_____	_____
			_____

Exercise Two

Identify a real personal or business situation in which you will need to communicate important information orally. This can be on the phone or in person. It can be a communication to one person or to multiple people. For instance, maybe you have your annual physical coming up and you want to remember to bring up three or four key points with the doctor. Use the *Loci* method to outline your key points. Attach each key point to a specific body part. On the drive to your doctor's appointment, rehearse your key points using the *Loci* method. Then see if you can get through the communication without using your notes.

Your Situation

Key Point	Body Part	Image
_____	_____	_____
_____	_____	_____
_____	_____	_____
_____	_____	_____
_____	_____	_____
_____	_____	_____
_____	_____	_____
_____	_____	_____
_____	_____	_____

Day Four: Colorful Categories
Skills: Chunking and Visualization
Number of Exercises: Two

There are many instances when our future To Do's involve holding a short list of items in memory so that we can execute a particular task. Usually we just write the items down on a piece of paper. Another approach is to start exercising our brain more by trying to hold short lists in memory. Of course, you may still want to keep a written list as a backup. Two mental skills that make it easy to keep short lists in memory are chunking and visualization. Divide items on a list into meaningful chunks of three to five items. Give each chunk a colorful label. Create a vivid and/or wacky image to go with the label to make it more memorable.

Example One

Annika needs to purchase several items at the supermarket for a dinner party she is giving. First she makes out her grocery list. Her list includes: *Parmesan cheese, oregano, pasta, basil, tomato sauce, oil and vinegar dressing, salad seasoning, Tabasco sauce, salt, pepper, hamburger, and sausage.* She proceeds to chunk the list and gives each chunk a colorful label. She sequences the chunks by supermarket aisle location. Then she creates a vivid image to go with each label. This helps imprint the labels in her memory. She holds the labels and images in her mind and uses them at the supermarket to remember which aisles she needs to go down. Once in the correct aisles, the shelf labels serve as memory joggers for the ingredients she needs to purchase.

Chunk	Label	Image
Pasta	Little Italy	Leaning Tower of Pisa toppling into the aisle
Parmesan cheese		
Tomato sauce		

Chunk	Label	Image
Tabasco sauce	Daring Dresser	Checkout cashier wearing a lacy, low-cut outfit
Oil and vinegar dressing		
Salad seasoning		
Oregano	Spicy Lover	Tall, dark, and handsome man pushing a grocery cart
Basil		
Salt		
Pepper		
Hamburger	Bovine Dancers	Spotted cow and pink pig dancing the jig
Sausage		

Example Two

Julia owns a successful dance studio for talented school-age children. Every summer she must get ready for the upcoming year by completing a myriad of tasks. To help her stay focused and keep from feeling overwhelmed, Julia breaks down the tasks into smaller chunks and gives each chunk a label. She can easily hold the labels in her mind and mentally check off the items.

Marketing
Create and mail out fall brochures
Get advertisements in local papers
Update business Web site

Scheduling
Schedule student performances
Schedule field trips to dance events
Schedule guest teachers

Curriculum
Work on new choreography
Create fall curriculum

Exercise One

Alex and his wife, who have just retired, are spending their first winter in Florida. They have made a list of the things to which they must attend before they leave their home in Vermont. Help them organize and reinforce their memory by chunking and labeling their list below into three or four groupings.

To Do   **Chunks & Labels**

Have mail forwarded

Stop the newspaper

Empty the refrigerator so perishables
don't spoil

Purchase an "Easy Pass" unit for the car

Lower the heat

Ask oil company to put you on
the automatic refill program

Get car serviced for the drive down

Turn off outside water valves
so pipes don't freeze

Arrange for someone to snowplow

Leave a key with a neighbor in
case of emergency

Make reservations at hotels in Virginia
and Georgia for the drive down

Notify the police to watch the house

Make sure alarm system is working

Put jewelry and important papers
in the bank safe

Put inside lights on automatic timers

Get AAA itinerary for the drive down

Exercise Two

Round One

You have been asked to handle the logistics for the upcoming annual sales meeting. Below is a list of things you must do. Study the list for three minutes, then cover the list and write down all the items you can remember.

Create participant roster _____

Send out welcome letter _____

Reserve hotel rooms for participants _____

Mail pre-work to participants _____

Put seminar materials in binders _____

Proofread seminar materials _____

Reserve conference room _____

Reserve audiovisual equipment _____

Set up the conference room _____

Arrange for daily catered lunches _____

Arrange for visitor passes _____

Confirm participant attendance via e-mail _____

Round Two

Study the chunked list on the left for thirty seconds. Then cover the list, and in the boxes on the right, write down the three labels. Then fill in as many items as you can under each label.

Seminar Materials

Proofread seminar materisl

Put seminar materials in binders

Mail seminar pre-work to participants

Create seminar participant roster

Label: _____

_____

_____

_____

_____

Participant Arrangements

Confirm participant attendance vis e-mail

Reserve hotel rooms for participants

Arrange for visitor passes

Send out welcome letter

Label: _____

_____

_____

_____

_____

Conference Room

Reserve conference room

Reserve audiovisual equipment

Put participant materials and
    name tents on tables

Arrange for daily catered lunches

Label: _____

_____

_____

_____

_____

---

*Note: How many labels did you remember? How many more items did you remember in Round Two?

Day Five: Powerful Pairs

Skills: Linking and Visualization
Number of Exercises: Three

One way to remember all of the items on your To Do list is to combine the items together through linked visual images:

1. Form a visual image for each item on the list.
2. Link the image for the first item with the image for the second item.
3. Link the image for the second item with the image for third item.
4. Continue until all the images on your list are visually linked into pairs.

Example One

Bernard, a highly visual learner, needs to pick up several items at the hardware store for the winter season. He visualizes each item on his list. Then he pairs the items and links the pairs together through colorful images, such that each image leads to the next item on the list. He heads off to the hardware store with the colorful images replaying in his mind. The items on his list are: *sand, candles, electric heater, rock salt,* and *windshield washer fluid*. Below are his linked images.

> a *sand* castle at dusk with *candles* glowing in the windows
> *candles* dripping sticky white wax on the red hot coils of the *electric heater*
> the red hot *electric heater* melting the *rock salt* into silvery puddles
> the melted *rock salt* being poured into the *windshield washer fluid* tank of his car

Example Two

One way to shorten a long list of items is to link the items into pairs through visual association. By doing this, a list of ten individual items becomes a list of five paired items. The key is to use strong and dynamic visual images for your linkages. The sillier the linkages the more memorable they will be. Here is an example of how this technique works.

Two Item List	**One Item List**
Deposit check	Give Sally your *check* as a *house gift*
Purchase gift for Sally's new home	
Pick up steaks at the butcher shop	Shoemaker uses the fat from the *steaks* to
Drop off shoes at the shoemaker	patch your *shoes*

Exercise One

Your daughter is getting married next June. Together you are planning a big, traditional wedding. Below is a list of the major things you and she must attend to prior to the wedding. Link the eight items on your list together through consecutive images, such that each image serves as a prompt for the next item on the list.

To Do List	**Image**
Reserve band	The *band* milling around the *reception hall*
Reserve reception hall	The *reception hall* being set up by the *caterer*
Find caterer	_____
Secure a florist	_____
Get wedding invitations	_____
Order the wedding cake	_____
Shop for wedding gown	_____
Hire videographer	_____
Create seating plan	_____
Buy gifts for bridesmaids	_____

Exercise Two

Below is a list of eight random items. Shorten the list to four visually paired items. Make your pairs memorable through exaggeration and humor. The first pairing has been done for you.

Item	Image
Banana	*1. The clown pretended to smoke the banana*
Clown	
Sidewalk	2. _____
Snowman	_____
Fair	3. _____
Cow	_____
Patch	4. _____
Criminal	_____

Exercise Three

Make a list of the daily chores you must accomplish. Then see if you can shorten the list and make it more memorable by creating dynamic visual pairs.

Chore	Image
_____	_____
_____	_____
_____	_____
_____	_____

Day Six: Storytelling
Skills: Verbalization, Visualization, and Linking
Number of Exercises: Two

Storytelling is a tradition that has been part of the human culture from the beginning of human civilization. Archeologists continue to find story drawings and symbols on the walls of ancient caves all over the world. The Old Testament stories date back to approximately 1400 B.C. In his epic poems *The Odyssey* and *The Illiad,* which date back to 800–600 B.C. Homer mentions bards, or singing minstrels, who wandered the countryside singing stories that captured the history of Greek mythology and the Greek people. In "memory"storytelling, you link unrelated items together in a simple and colorful tale. The memory skills used to create a "memory story" include *linking, visualization,* and *verbalization.* Visualize the items to be remembered, and link them to a vivid image. Weave items to be remembered into a simple and colorful story.

Example One
You wake up in the middle of the night remembering that you promised to bring props to play rehearsal tomorrow night. Rather than get out of bed, you turn to the storytelling method. The props you promised to bring include candlesticks, a flower basket, a broomstick, and a watering can. To reinforce these items in your memory, you make up the following story. You envision the clumsy male lead knocking over the *candlesticks,* which set fire to the *flower basket.* The director tries to put out the fire by swatting at it with the *broomstick,* which also catches fire. The leading lady saves the day by pouring water from the *watering can* onto the flames.

Example Two
Tom is a landscaper. On the way to his first job he must remember to bring his ladder and work gloves, as well as pick up coffee and donuts for the crew. He forms a colorful image of the key items he must remember and weaves them together in this silly story . . . The crew climbs up the *ladder* to the roof of the *donut* shop, where they enjoy the view and their morning *coffee* break. Because the *coffee* is hot, they wear *gloves* to keep from burning their hands.

Exercise One

You are planning your husband's fiftieth birthday party. You want to have the following items on hand. Make up an imaginative story that links the items together. Feel free to make inanimate objects come alive.

Items

Black and gold balloons
"Over the Hill" sign
Baby pictures of your husband
Streamers
Exploding cigars

Wondering how to get started? Here is one beginning: *The birthday boy is wearing diapers and puffing on a cigar when . . . .*

Your Birthday Story

Exercise Two

As you are driving into work, your business partner calls your cell phone and asks if you would pick up the following items on your way in to work: *stamps*, an *extension cord*, a *picture frame*, and *nails*. As you drive, you make up a funny and fanciful story, linking the items together. Write your story in the space below

Your Story

Day Seven: Hot Potato

Skill: Linking
Number of Exercises: Two

Sometimes you are thrown a memory "hot potato." This is a quick hand-off of items to be remembered, tossed to you while you are on the run or multitasking. A quick and easy memory skill for handling these urgencies is *first-letter linking.* Use the first letters of the items to be remembered to create or make up a memorable word (*acronym*), or use the first letters of the items to be remembered to create a memorable sentence (*acrostic*).

Example One

Your mom calls your cell phone at work in the middle of a meeting. She's not feeling well and wants you to bring her *soup, saltines, Popsicles,* and a *thermometer* on your way home from work. You make a quick mental note of the first letter of the items your mom wants . . . SSPT. While your boss is finishing his presentation, you mentally turn the letters into an abbreviated, acrostic sentence . . . *Shame Sick Pickup Things.* You'll use your sentence as a prompt at the end of the day to remind you to pick up the soup, saltines, Popsicles, and a thermometer.

Example Two

Your mom calls back two hours later. She is feeling worse and wants to add some items to the list. She would like to add *aspirin, suckers,* and *Kleenex.* Once again you use first-letter linking and quickly come up with the acronym *ASK.* You'll use your acrostic and your acronym at the pharmacy to remember the items you need to purchase.

Exercise One

Below are a series of memory hot potatoes that are tossed your way. Read each hot potato request and see how quickly you can turn the request into an acronym or an acrostic.

Hot Potato Requests

1. You are on the golf course when your wife calls and asks you to pick up hairspray, toothpaste, and eye solution.

_____

_____

_____

2. You're in the car when your son calls with an urgent request. He needs you to pick up computer paper, an ink cartridge, and pens so he can finish his college application essay.

_____

_____

_____

3. Your boss calls from the airport and asks you to cancel his afternoon meeting with the vice presidents from finance, engineering, marketing, and sales.

_____

_____

_____

Exercise Two

Make up a list of three to six top-priority items you need to attend to this week. Use first-letter linking to turn your list into an acronym or an acrostic.

Your List   **Acronym/Acrostic**

_____   _____

                        _____

_____   _____

                        _____

_____   _____

                        _____

_____   _____

                        _____

_____   _____

Dr. Brainfit's Advice Column

Dear Dr. Brainfit,

I know many people who take ginkgo biloba on a regular basis as an anti-dote for memory decline. Personally, I'm skeptical of herbal supplements that have not been approved by the FDA. What does the research say about ginkgo biloba?

Henry from Atlanta

Dear Henry,

Ginkgo biloba is a tree with a very long and interesting history of medical applications. Here are the facts to date:

Ginkgo Biloba and Memory

Ginkgo (Ginkgo biloba) is one of the oldest living species of trees. The ginkgo biloba extract used in herbal supplements comes from the leaves of the ginkgo tree. The Chinese have long believed that ginkgo slows down the aging process and contributes to longevity. Traditionally ginkgo has been used to enhance memory and treat circulatory problems. Ginkgo biloba is one of the most extensively studied botanicals in use today. In Europe, ginkgo biloba extract is one of the most popular and best-selling herbal medications on the market. In France and Germany, where it is available by prescription only, it ranks in the top five of all prescriptions written.

In recent years, a number of reports on the efficacy of ginkgo biloba have appeared in the *Journal of the American Medical Association*. As with many herbal supplements, the research studies are sometimes contradictory and not conclusive. However, ginkgo biloba does have some potent attributes that appear to promote brain health. An article on the University of Maryland

▼

Medicine Web site concludes that ginkgo biloba extract may be especially effective in patients with age-related dementia resulting from decreased blood flow to the brain. Laboratory studies have shown that ginkgo biloba extract improves blood flow by dilating blood vessels and reducing blood viscosity. Additionally, the ginkgo leaves appear to contain potent antioxidant properties. Antioxidants are substances that scavenge free radicals, which are compounds that can alter and damage brain cells. The article mentions a clinical study in which Alzheimer's patients taking ginkgo biloba extract showed improvement in tasks involving memory (such as remembering names of relatives and daily activities), as well as in social behavior and reduced feelings of depression. In clinical studies involving healthy adults, memory gains were cited but appeared to be more short-term in nature. It may be that ginkgo biloba, with its ability to improve blood circulation and fight free radicals, works best in healthy adults in slowing brain aging, rather than significantly boosting memory.[1]

Chapter Six

Remembering How Many

"Not everything that can be counted counts,
and not everything that counts can be counted."
—ALBERT EINSTEIN

Numbers Make the World Go Round

There is no escaping it. Numbers are a requirement of modern living. If you don't believe it, think of all the instances in which your everyday activities require you to use numbers. Try to get basic services or accomplish a simple transaction without providing numerical information. If you don't have one or more of the following identification numbers it's unlikely you will get very far:

- home telephone number
- billing zip code
- credit card number
- account number
- policy number
- product code number

- registration number
- reservation number
- security code number
- social security number

It's easy to envision a time when all you'll need to accomplish basic services will be your appropriate identification number and a computer outlet. For example, take the current self-service check-out lines at the supermarket: a computer scans the product codes and prices of your groceries. Your purchase totals appear on a screen. You push *yes* to approve the total, enter your credit card, and *presto* the transaction is completed. The only thing missing is the robot to bag your groceries and wish you a pleasant day.

Remembering Numbers

So what's a nonnumbers person to do? How do we organize, file, and retrieve all these important numbers? Perhaps in the future, all that will be required is our thumbprint pressed on a scanner, which will activate a search of our identification numbers and match the right number to the right transaction.

Working with numbers is a specific type of brain activity. If we no longer use this brain function, our ability to remember and work with numbers will, over time, become less reliable and agile. I once asked a group of seniors if they wanted me to show them how to balance their checking accounts using computer-based online banking. They politely said, "No, thank you." When I asked several of them why not, I was surprised by their response. It was not learning the new technology that concerned them; rather, they were concerned about losing their mental agility with numbers. For these seniors, mentally balancing their checking accounts was the only numbers-based activity they engaged in on a regular basis.

Memory Tips for Remembering Numbers

1. Split large numbers into smaller, manageable chunks.
2. Replace abstract numbers with concrete images.

3. Link images together in a silly picture or a story.
4. Look for familiar patterns or associations among numbers.
5. Play games that involve remembering numbers.
6. Experiment with your favorite number association code on a regular basis, in everyday situations.
7. Use external memory aids and technology to help you organize, store, and access important numbers.
8. Spend time learning about real life codes (semaphores, Braille, Morse code, ancient Greek number codes, and others).
9. Select a code that interests you; see if you can learn the code.
10. See movies and read novels that involve breaking a code.

What's the Workout Rationale?

Unless you are someone who works with numbers on a daily basis, numbers are tough to remember because they are intangible, difficult to visualize, and possess no inherent meaning. If we are going to build our mental stamina when it comes to remembering numbers, we will need a way to infuse numbers with concrete meaning. A popular approach to remembering numbers involves using codes that convert numbers into meaningful associations. These codes can be visual, verbal, or mathematical.

Codes are used in many different applications. Examples of codes in use today include Morse code, Braille, and the ASCII computer code. Some religious traditions, like Kabbalah, hold that God used codes to hide important messages in the Bible and other religious documents. The U.S. Department of Defense is actively seeking individuals who can decode the messages of Islamic terrorists. If you liked the book *The Da Vinci Code*, you will enjoy playing with the number codes in this chapter.

Let's Work Out!

Welcome to the **Remembering How Many** fitness station. As a result of your participation in this week's workout, you'll increase your aptitude for remembering the important numbers in your life. You'll use select memory skills to make remembering numbers simple and fun.

Weekly Exercise Planner

The following table lays out the *Brainfit* workout for **Remembering How Many**. Each day's workout exercises will be preceded by an Exercise Introduction, which previews the memory skills to be used for the day, and provides examples of how the skills will be applied in the exercises.

Day	Exercise Name	Memory Skill	Pages
Day One	Free Association	Linking	136–138
Day Two	Fixed Association	Linking	139–141
Day Three	Pictures This	Visualization Linking	142–145
Day Four	Seeing Patterns	Visualization	146–147
Day Five	Rhythm & Rhyme	Verbalization Visualization Linking	148–150
Day Six	Alphabet Soup	Verbalization Linking	151–154
Day Seven	Mixed Bag	Multiple Skills	155–156

Day One: Free Association

Skill: Linking

Number of Exercises: Three

Some numbers already have inherent meaning for us, based on our personal biography and cultural history. For instance, most people easily remember numbers associated with their birth day, month, and year, and can easily remember numbers associated with important historical or social events. So, when you need to remember an important number in your life, it makes sense to link it to numbers the brain already finds meaningful.

Example One

In order to enter the marina where her sailboat is docked, Chloe must punch in a number code. The code is changed each year for security purposes. The numerical code this year is 8036. Chloe first chunks the number into two chunks, 80 and 36, then searches for familiar associations. The first association is easy. Her grandfather is in his eighties, and he is the one who taught her how to sail. For the second association, she uses a little imagination and humor. The number thirty-six is the bust size Chloe wishes she had.

Example Two

Carlos bases his ATM (automated teller machine) code on his dog's birthday. His dog was born on New Year's Eve, 2001. Carlos inserts this familiar date into his six-digit ATM code, ending up with the number 12-31-01. This is a number that is easy for him to remember.

Example Three

Louisa is a history buff and often uses historical associations to help her remember important phone numbers. For example, her doctor's phone number is 391-1900. To help her secure this number in memory, Louisa chunks the number and then links the chunked numbers to well known historical dates.

Number	Historical Association
39	Year World War II began
1	Adolph Hitler . . . *one* name most associated with World War II
1900	Century in which World War II occurred

Exercise One

Take a look at the following random numbers. Your task is to find as many numbers as you can that have familiar associations for you. The first number has been chunked and associations have been provided to serve as an example.

Number	Chunk	Free Association
0074755890	*007*	*James Bond's secret service number is 007*
	74	*First child was born in 1974*
	747	*A super jet model is the 747*
	55	*Distinctly middle-aged*
	890	*Grandmother is 89, Grandfather is 90*
3486921750	_____	_____
	_____	_____
	_____	_____
	_____	_____
	_____	_____
9746351082	_____	_____
	_____	_____
	_____	_____
	_____	_____
	_____	_____
96352107401	_____	_____
	_____	_____
	_____	_____
	_____	_____
	_____	_____

Exercise Two

Security experts tell us that the most secure codes contain both letters and numbers. Create a security code for your new home wall safe. The code should be six to eight characters long and contain both letters and numbers. The number and letter chunks should have personal meaning for you.

Code	Association
_____	_____
_____	_____

Exercise Three

Insert your own personal numbers below. Then see how many familiar associations you can find in each number.

Type of Code	Number	Association
Social Security	_____	_____
Zip Code	_____	_____
Doctor's Telephone	_____	_____
Credit Card	_____	_____

Day Two: Fixed Association
Skill: Linking
Number of Exercises: Two

In addition to **free associations**, we can also create **fixed associations** to better remember numbers. The advantage of fixed associations is that they can be memorized and used repeatedly. Over time, your brain begins to naturally substitute the fixed associations for the abstract numbers themselves, creating strong memory tracers. Here is the process for creating a fixed association number code.

1. Create fixed associations for the numbers 1 through 12.
2. Select fixed associations that have concrete imagery.
3. Link the fixed association images together in a story or picture.

Example One
Here is an example of someone's fixed association code. You will use this code in today's exercises. Study the numbers and their fixed associations. See how quickly you can memorize the code.

Number	Fixed Association
0	Hollow log
1	Penny
2	Twins
3	Triplets
4	Baseball diamond (4 corners)
5	Fingers
6	Six-pack
7	Dwarfs
8	V8 juice
9	Baseball team
10	Bowling pins
11	Snake eyes (dice)
12	Dozen eggs

Example Two

To remember his locker number at the Health Club, Randall uses the fixed association code to create a silly, but memorable story. His locker number is 2103. Here are the steps he follows using the fixed association code presented in Example One.

1. Chunk the numbers 2 - 10 - 3.
2. Convert the numbers to their fixed association images.
>   2 = Twins
>   10 = Bowling pins
>   3 = Triplets
3. Create a story that links the fixed association images together.
   The twins (2) went bowling (10) with the triplets (3).

Exercise One

Using the fixed association code presented in Example One, try to decode the numbers embedded in the phrases below. Check your responses against the answers at the end of the chapter.

a. The happy dwarfs split a six-pack with Snow White.
b. The twins crawled through the hollow log and found a penny each.
c. The baseball team ate a dozen eggs and washed them down with V8 juice.
d. The triplets knocked down all the bowling pins and won a penny each.
e. The bowling pins crushed the fingers of the triplets.

Exercise Two

In this exercise you'll see how using fixed associations can boost your memory of numbers. This is a two-part exercise. In Part One, you'll try to remember a series of numbers without the aid of a fixed association code. In Part Two, you'll try to remember a series of numbers using a fixed association code.

Part One

Study the series of numbers below for one minute. Do not try to apply the fixed association code yet. Then cover all of the numbers in the series and write down as many numbers as you can remember.

98
26
12
65
34

Part Two

Now substitute fixed association images for each of the numbers which follow. Link the images together in a wacky story or phrase. Write your story or phrase to the right of each number. Then study the stories and phrases you created for one minute. Cover the numbers and their corresponding stories/phrases. Write down all the numbers you can remember.

Number	Fixed Association
79	The seven dwarfs play baseball.
11	_____
65	_____
81	_____
30	_____
12	_____

How did you do? If you're like most people, you remembered more numbers using the fixed association code. The more you work with fixed associations, the easier and faster it will be for you to remember the important numbers in your life.

Day Three: Picture This
Skills: Visualization and Linking
Number of Exercises: Three

Some numbers have built-in imagery. When you look at these numbers, they resemble familiar images and shapes. We can capitalize on this built-in imagery and use it to create a picture association code. To create a picture code, associate numbers with the concrete images they look like. Link the images together in a wacky story or phrase.

Example One

Wendy recently passed her real estate license exam. She is excited to begin her new profession. She is wonderful with people and a creative marketer. She has one small drawback: she is terrible at remembering numbers, which is a definite problem in her field. So Wendy decides to try a new approach to remembering numbers. She makes up a picture association code to help her better remember quotes and home prices. To create her picture code, Wendy converts the numbers zero through ten to the concrete images they look like. She even sketches a few of the images. Then, she commits the code to memory. Try to commit Wendy's picture association code to memory, as you will need to use it in the exercises that follow.

Wendy's Picture Association Code

Number	Picture
0	Egg
1	Candle
2	Swan
3	Ocean wave
4	Sailboat
5	Diver
6	Rattlesnake
7	Diving board
8	Snowman
9	Balloon on a string
10	Bat & Ball

Wendy's Sketches

Example Two

Lynn, Wendy's younger sister, uses Wendy's picture code to remember the number of her school locker, which is 4529. Here is the process she follows:

1. Convert each number to its picture association image
   - 4 = sailboat
   - 5 = diver
   - 2 = swan
   - 9 = balloon
2. Link images together in a picture or a story.
3. Add color and/or humor to make the images and their story connections more vivid.

Using the process above, here is the picture Lynn creates in her mind's eye: *a silver sailboat (4) with a diver (5) on deck who is loading on scuba gear. Following the sailboat is a black swan (2) with a red balloon (9) tied around its neck. The diver is going to rescue the swan.*

Exercise One

Using Wendy's picture association code, convert the images below into the numbers they represent. The first one is done for you. Try to complete the exercise from memory.

Image	What is the number?
a. *Diving board, Wave, Rattlesnake*	*736*
b. Snowman, Sailboat, Balloon	_____
c. Candle, Diver, Swan, Egg	_____
d. Balloon, Wave, Wave, Sailboat	_____
e. Candle, Diving Board, Swan	_____
f. Rattlesnake, Bat & Ball, Sailboat	_____

Exercise Two

Use the picture association code to create a picture, phrase or wacky story to help you remember the following numbers. The first one is done for you.

Number	Association
348	*A wave rocking a sailboat with a melting snowman on deck*
105	_____
019	_____
108	_____
3520	_____
8697	_____
05739	_____

Exercise Three

Use the picture association code to convert your important personal numbers into images. Link the images together in a wacky phrase or story.

Your Number	Image	Phrase/Story
_____	_____	_____
License	_____	_____
	_____	_____
_____	_____	_____
Social Security	_____	_____
	_____	_____
_____	_____	_____
Checking Account	_____	_____
	_____	_____

Day Four: Seeing Patterns

Skill: Visualization

Number of Exercises: Two

Some numbers have inherent patterns to them. Many numbers have mathematical relationships that are familiar. Other numbers are presented in ways that suggest sequential or spatial patterns. Recognizing these familiar patterns provides a memory hook we can use to secure numbers in long-term memory. Look for spatial, sequential, and mathematical patterns in a number display.

Example One

Julia's new business phone number is 864-0246. Since Julia is pretty good at math, she immediately sees a simple mathematical pattern. The *exchange* (864) is arrived at by subtracting 2 from each preceding number. The *line number* (0246) is arrived at by adding two to each preceding number. She also notes that 64 and 46 are reverse patterns.

Example Two

Hassan is having trouble remembering the telephone number of his college advisor. The number is 369-5689. Looking at the location of the numbers on a telephone keypad,

however, Hassan sees two visual shapes. The numbers 369 form a vertical line on the keypad. The numbers 5689 form a square. Now every time he dials the number, Hassan focuses on these two patterns. With little effort, he soon secures the number in memory.

Exercise One

Make up a telephone number for your new fax line in which all of the numbers have a mathematical relationship.

Telephone Number

_____	_____	_____
Area code	Exchange	Line number

Exercise Two

Select three telephone numbers you would like to commit to memory. Look at the telephone keypad in Example Two on page 146. See if you can find memorable patterns or shapes in any part of the numbers.

Telephone Number   **Pattern/Shape**

_____   _____

_____   _____

_____   _____

Day Five: Rhythm & Rhyme

Skills: Verbalization, Visualization, and Linking
Number of Exercises: Three

When we rhyme numbers, we create sound patterns that imprint on our memory. Creating number rhymes is a fun and easy way for auditory learners to boost their memory of numbers. Here's how it works:

1. Create a rhyming association code in which each number is replaced by a rhyming word with a concrete image.
2. Select rhyming words that represent concrete images.
3. Link the images together in a silly story.

Example One

Henry has a college chemistry class he loathes. His locker in the chemistry lab is number 4238. He remembers his locker number by repeating the following rhyming phrase:

Four – Two – Three – Eight,
Which class do I really hate?

Example Two

Patty's new piano teacher lives on the sixth floor in apartment 623. The piano piece Patty is currently practicing is the "The Flight of the Bumblebee," by composer Rimsky-Korsakov. To remember her piano teacher's apartment number, she creates this rhyme:

Playing "Flight of the Bumblebee"
Requires entering apartment 623.

Example Three

Mary Jane creates a rhyming association code that she commits to memory. She uses the rhymes to create stories that help her remember important numbers. Below is the rhyming association code she creates.

Number	Rhyming Word
0	Hero
1	Sun
2	Shoe
3	Bee
4	Door
5	Hive
6	Sticks
7	Heaven
8	Gate
9	Wine
10	Hen

Mary Jane wants to purchase a new printer for her computer. The model number for this printer is 003549. Using her rhyming association code, she converts the numbers to their rhyming words, and links the words together in this silly story:

Two heroes (00) are pursued by an angry bee (3) from a nearby honey hive (5). The heroes run through the door (4) of their house and celebrate their escape with a glass of wine (9).

Exercise One

Study the rhyming association code in Example Three. Then see how quickly you can decode the numbers embedded in the following phrases.

1. The angry boy kicked the *gate* with his *shoe* and hit the bee*hive* with some *sticks*.
2. For heaven's sake, how many times do I have to tell you to take off your shoes and close the door behind you?
3. The bee landed on the gate, rested for a few minutes in the sunshine and then flew back to the hive.

4. The wine spilled on her shoe. The bee was drawn to its sweetness, but she flicked it away with some sticks.

5. The hen drank the wine and went to heaven on a sunny day.

Exercise Two

Use the rhyming association code to convert each number into its image association. Then link the images together in a silly phrase or story

Number	Rhyming Words	Phrase/Story
28	_____	_____
103	_____	_____
64	_____	_____
17	_____	_____
9	_____	_____

Exercise Three

Select three important phone numbers you would like to remember better, which you have not committed to memory. Use the rhyming association code. Convert the phone number to its corresponding rhyming word images. Link the images together in a silly phrase or story. Then dial the phone number using only that phrase or story as your memory prompt.

Number	Rhyming Words	Phrase/Story
_____	_____	_____
_____	_____	_____
_____	_____	_____

Day Six: Alphabet Soup

Skill: Verbalization and Linking
Number of Exercises: Three

As you've seen, there are many different ways to create number codes. One type of code we haven't looked at yet is the *alphabet association code.* In this approach, numbers are converted to letters of the alphabet. Letters are then linked together to form memorable words, acronyms, and acrostics.

Example One

On a typical telephone keypad, each number, with the exception of the numbers 1 and 0, has three or four letters printed above it. These alphabet letters can be converted into words and acrostics making it easier to remember certain telephone numbers.

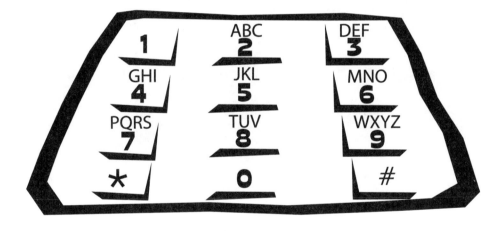

Phone Numbers	Words
520 – 3463	JAZ – FINE
786 – 3425	RUN – DICK

Example Two

Gerald's sister has just moved to a new state. Gerald uses the alphabet in the telephone keypad to create an acrostic that will help him to remember his sister's new area code.

Area Code	Corresponding Letters	Acrostic
422	HBC	Help Brother Call

Example Three

Telephone numbers are not the only numbers we need to remember. Often we need to remember numbers without the aid of the telephone keypad. The process below illustrates how you can create your own freestanding alphabet association code. This approach is popular for remembering multidigit numbers. Here's how it works:

Step One:

Convert numbers to letters of the alphabet to create an alphabet association code.
1 = A, 2 = B, 3 = C, 4 = D, 5 = E, 6 = F, 7 = G, 8 = H, 9 = I, and 0 = J

Step Two:

Chunk large numbers into pairs.
2372 is chunked into two pairs, 23 and 72

Step Three:

Convert each pair of numbers into letters using the alphabet association code in Step One.
23 = BC
72 = GB

Step Four:

Treat the resulting letters as name initials. Think of famous people who fit these initials.
23 = Bill Clinton
72 = George Burns

Step Five:

Find an association that links the famous people together in a picture or a story.
Bill Clinton and George Burns puffing on cigars, telling jokes.

Exercise One

Use the telephone keypad as your alphabet association code and create acronyms or acrostics for the following Massachusetts telephone area codes. For the number 1, substitute the letter I and for the number 0, substitute the letter O. The first two are done for you as examples.

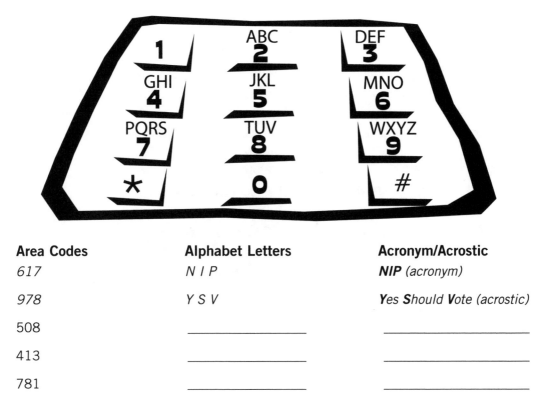

Area Codes	Alphabet Letters	Acronym/Acrostic
617	*N I P*	**NIP** *(acronym)*
978	*Y S V*	**Y**es **S**hould **V**ote *(acrostic)*
508	_____	_____
413	_____	_____
781	_____	_____

Exercise Two

People often use the telephone keypad as their alphabet association code to create memorable business phone numbers. For example, a children's theater might choose the business number 1-800-543-2287, which becomes 1-800-KID ACTS.

Now imagine that you are starting the new business you always dreamed of having. Create a few new business telephone numbers that translate into a meaningful marketing message for your new business.

Business Telephone Number   **Marketing Message**

_____   _____

Exercise Three

Use the alphabet code process described in Example Three on page 152 to convert the following multidigit numbers into the initials of famous people. Link the famous people together in a memorable picture. The first number has been converted for you as an example. Your task is to complete the last two columns (*names, association*) for each of the numbers below. If you like, turn this into a parlor game with friends. Get teams to compete against one another. See which team can come up with names and associations the fastest.

Partial Alphabet Association Code

1 = A 2 = B 3 = C 4 = D 5 = E 6 = F 7 = G 8 = H 9 = I 0 = J

Number	Chunks	Initials	Names	Association
0022	*00, 22*	*J.J.& B.B.*	*Janet Jackson*	*Wardrobe*
			Bill Blass	*Malfunction*
a. 7338	73, 38	G.C. & C.H.	_____	_____
			_____	_____
b. 0412	04, 12	J.D. & A.B.	_____	_____
			_____	_____
c. 3372	33, 72	C.C. & G.B.	_____	_____
			_____	_____
d. 8643	86, 43	H.F. & D.C.	_____	_____
			_____	_____
e. 9681	96, 81	I.F. & H.A.	_____	_____
			_____	_____

Day Seven: Mixed Bag
Skill: Multiple Skills
Number of Exercises: Two

The exercises for Day Seven ask you to draw on memory techniques and skills applied in previous exercises.

Exercise One
Review all of the different approaches for remembering numbers in this week's workout exercises. Then select the memory association code you like the best. Practice remembering numbers using your selected code on a regular basis in the following everyday situations. Each week pick a different situation from the list as your practice focus. Feel free to add your own practice opportunities to the list. The more you practice using the memory code, the more ingrained it will become. Pretty soon remembering numbers will be a breeze.

Practice Situations
- Prices of things you buy
- Travel information
- Flight numbers
- Train numbers
- Bus numbers
- Street addresses
- Highway exits
- Clock time
- TV and radio stations
- Your weight
- License plate of a "road rage" driver
- Dates
- Check numbers and amounts
- Golf and bowling scores
- Card games
- Telephone numbers

Exercise Two

For this exercise, you will need to preselect either the picture association code or the rhyming association code. You'll be playing the old memory game known as "Concentration," using your selected association code. The game provides a fun way to learn an association code by heart. You will need a complete deck of playing cards. Here are the game instructions:

1. First shuffle the cards and place them face down on a flat surface.
2. Pick up any two cards at once.
3. When you find a match, call out the appropriate code association. For example, if you draw two 6s, you will call out "two snakes," using the picture association code. If you do not call out the correct code association, it does not count as a match and you must return the cards to their original position.
4. Pull the cards you successfully matched and coded out of the deck and set them aside.
5. The game ends when you have made matches of all the cards in the deck.

Dr. Brainfit's Advice Column

Dear Dr. Brainfit,

There seems to be a lot of interest in the media recently about the health benefits of red wine. I'm not much of a drinker, but I'm considering drinking a glass of red wine a day. What is the effect of red wine on the brain and memory?

Harry from Oklahoma City

Dear Harry,

You're right, Harry. Red wine has received lots of positive press. Still, few doctors would suggest that someone who doesn't drink start drinking. Alcohol is a known brain toxin. Any decision to start drinking, even moderate amounts of red wine, should be based on facts and a doctor's review of your personal medical history.

Red Wine and the Brain

A number of research studies suggest that a daily glass or two of red wine may help protect against neurodegenerative disorders such as Parkinson's and Alzheimer's. It is not the alcohol in the wine, though, that provides the health benefits. The health benefits are derived from the antioxidant properties in the red wine, in particular resveratrol. The results of a recent research study conducted by Dr. Egemen Savaskan at the University of Basel in Switzerland showed that resveratrol protected cells against beta-amyloid oxidative damage by mopping up cell-damaging free radicals.[1] Another research study conducted at the University of Milan discovered that neural cells will regenerate when exposed to resveratrol. The researchers in this study suggest that a glass or two of red wine a day can help reinforce neural connections sevenfold and prevent further degeneration. Resveratrol can also be found in grapes, various berries, and peanuts. Some health food outlets even offer resveratrol in capsule form as a nutritional supplement.[2]

While the resveratrol in red wine offers a number of health benefits, including possible protection against stroke and heart disease, it is important to keep in mind that alcohol is a known brain toxin. Studies have shown that cognitive abilities are affected by even small amounts of alcohol. Alcohol affects many parts of the brain, but the most vulnerable cells are those associated with memory, attention, sleep, coordination, and judgment. Excessive and long-term alcohol use can lead to brain shrinkage, memory loss, and personality changes. So, to ensure you reap the benefits of red wine without the brain-damaging effects of alcohol, moderation is key. In the United States, moderate drinking is described as one glass of wine per day for women and two glasses of wine for men.

Solutions

Day Two, Exercise One: a. 76 b. 201 c. 9128 d. 3101 e. 1053

Day Three, Exercise One: b. 849, c. 1520, d. 9334, e. 172, f. 6104

Day Five, Exercise One: 1. 8256, 2. 724, 3. 3815, 4. 9236, 5. 10971

Day Six, Exercise Three (possible name associations): a) George Clooney, Charlton Heston; b) Johnny Depp, Alec Baldwin; c) Courteney Cox, George Bush; d) Henry Ford, Dick Clark; e) Ian Fleming, Hank Aaron; f) Bob Hope, Bing Crosby

Chapter Seven

Remembering
When

"Marriage is an alliance between two people,
one of whom never remembers birthdays,
and the other who never forgets."
—Ogden Nash

Special Occasions

Keeping track of special occasions and important events should be easy. After all, every-body has access to a calendar and many of us have electronic organizers. Yet forgetting anniversaries and birthdays is a frequently mentioned relationship stressor. Why is this? The answer by now is probably becoming obvious.

Remembering anniversaries, birthdays, and other calendar-based events poses a double memory challenge. First, we are dealing with numbers. Numbers, as you'll recall, are abstract and without inherent meaning. Second, we are dealing with future inten-tions that are often way out in time and occur only once or twice a year—as opposed to occurring on a routine basis. Memory retrieval cues for these future events will need to be time-based and event-based. Time-based retrieval cues are challenging: knowing that your anniversary is in July does not guarantee you'll remember the exact date in July, and knowing the exact date in July does not guarantee the date won't slip your mind.

Memory Tips For
Remembering When

1. Use a calendar and check it daily.
2. Get an electronic calendar with reminder feature, such as Microsoft Outlook.
3. Buy special occasion cards in advance and file them by month.
4. Develop and stick to a weekly schedule for routine tasks.
5. Place visual reminders, in your car or in a prominent place in your home.
6. Ask your doctor's office to mail you a reminder card for your next appointment.
7. Seek out medical clinics that use computerized calling to remind you of your upcoming appointments.
8. Schedule annual check-ups at the same time each year.
9. Ask friends and family to call and remind you of special occasions and agree to extend the same courtesy to them.

What's the Workout Rationale?

For calendar-based future events, your best bet will always be a paper calendar or an electronic organizer, preferably with an automatic reminder feature. Still, it is useful to know how to create your own memory cues, which can serve as backup memory triggers. After all, even with calendars it is possible to overlook an important date—so the more memory hooks the better. Also, actively using mental skills instead of depending on passive reminders provides the brain with healthy stimulation.

Let's Work Out!

Welcome to the **Remembering When** fitness station. As a result of your participation in this week's workout station, you'll strengthen your capacity for remembering the important dates in your life. You'll use select memory skills to strengthen your ability to remember birthdays, anniversaries, and special occasions in a timely manner. Using these techniques will help you store important dates in long-term memory and recall them as needed.

Weekly Exercise Planner

The following table lays out the *Brainfit* workout for **Remembering When.** Each day's exercises will be preceded by an Exercise Introduction, which previews the skills to be used for the day and provides examples of how the skills will be applied in the exercises.

Day	Exercise Name	Skill	Pages
Day One	Calendar Links	Linking	162–164
Day Two	Calendar Rhymes	Verbalization Linking	165–166
Day Three	Calendar Images	Visualization Verbalization Linking	167–169
Day Four	Environmental Prompts	Active Observation Visualization Linking	170–172
Day Five	Date Links	Visualization	173–174
Day Six	Calendar Chores	Linking Visualization	175–176
Day Seven	Calendar Accessories	Linking	177–178

Day One: Calendar Links

Skill: Linking

Number of Exercises: Two

First-letter linking is a quick and easy way to remember *what* we have to do *when*. In first-letter linking we connect an event to the calendar day when it occurs. Combine the first letters of the event with the first letter of the calendar day to create a memorable word (*acronym*). Combine the first letters of the event with the first letter of the calendar day to create a memorable sentence (*acrostic*).

Example One

Luis receives a reminder call on Friday from his dentist's office. He has an appointment for a cleaning with Dr. Mack next Monday. He combines the first letter of the doctor's name with the first letter of the calendar day and comes up with this easy-to-remember acronym.

Appointment	Acronym
Mack on Monday	MOM

Example Two

Julia remembers on Tuesday that she is supposed to pick up her new contact lenses on Wednesday. She combines the first letters of the event with the first letter of the calendar day to come up with the following fun acrostic.

Event	Acrostic
Contact Lenses on Wednesday	Californians love water

Example Three

Andrew likes to stick to routines. For instance, he always pays his bills on Friday and goes to the supermarket on Saturday. He thinks it will be easier for his mom, who is becoming a little forgetful, to follow a set schedule of weekly events. So he devises the following "linking" calendar for his mom, who is still mentally sharp when it comes to reading and word games.

Day	Event	First-Letter Link
Monday	Bills	**B**
Tuesday	Supermarket	**S**
Wednesday	Trash	**T**
Thursday	Laundry	**L**
Friday	Water aerobics	**W**

Then Andrew and his mom, whose name is Beth, create the following acrostic sentence to help Beth stick to the weekly routine. Using the first letters of the weekly events in calendar sequence, they come up with this acrostic sentence: "*Beth still takes long walks.*" Beth promises Andrew she will rehearse the memory sentence and stick to the weekly routine.

Exercise One

Make up an easy-to-remember acronym or acrostic for events you have coming up this week. The first entry is an example.

Event/Appointment	Acronym/Acrostic
Class on Tuesday	COT
_____	_____
_____	_____
_____	_____
_____	_____
_____	_____
_____	_____
_____	_____
_____	_____
_____	_____

Exercise Two

Make up a "linking" calendar for your own weekly routine (e.g., trash day, pay bills, mow lawn, bridge group, and others). List the routine events that make up your week in Column B. List one major event per day. Write the first letter of each event in Column C. Combine the letters in Column C, in vertical sequence, to create a memorable acrostic or acronym.

A. Day of Week	B. Routine Event	C. First-Letter Link
Monday	_____	_____
Tuesday	_____	_____
Wednesday	_____	_____
Thursday	_____	_____
Friday	_____	_____

Day Two: Calendar Rhymes

Skills: Verbalization and Linking

Number of Exercises: Two

For people who like working with words and word sounds, special calendar events can be fun to remember using simple rhymes. Create simple, childlike rhymes that link to special calendar events.

Example One

Katie's sister and dad both have birthdays that fall on the week of September twentieth. Katie, an English major, makes up the following rhyme to boost her memory of these important calendar events. She rehearses the rhyme once a week leading up to the events.

Remember the twentieth of September,

For birthdays of sister and dad,

These important dates I will remember,

So I don't make my loved ones sad.

Example Two

Don and Beverly are newlyweds. They want to make sure they never forget their wedding anniversary, which is August eleventh. Together they make up the following rhyme.

Our important date is August eleven

For rings, weddings, and vows,

It is the day of our own little heaven,

And we shall remember it now.

Exercise One

To create calendar rhymes, it helps to first come up with phrases that rhyme with each calendar month. Then you simply insert the rhyming phrase into your special events poem. The rhyming chart below has been started for you. The words that rhyme with each month are highlighted in bold. Create a rhyming phrase for the remaining calendar months.

Month	Rhyming Line
January	*If I forget this date it will be **scary***
February	*In this month I must be **wary***
March	_____
April	_____
May	_____
June	_____
July	_____
August	_____
September	_____
October	_____
November	_____
December	_____

Exercise Two

Think of the birthdays or anniversaries of three important people in your life. Then create rhyming poems which will help you better remember these special calendar dates. Insert the rhyming phrases you created in Exercise One to help you complete your poems.

Special Events   **Poems**

_____   _____

_____   _____

_____   _____

_____   _____

_____   _____

_____   _____

_____   _____

_____   _____

_____   _____

_____   _____

Day Three: Calendar Images

Skills: Visualization, Verbalization, and Linking
Number of Exercises: Two

Appointments and meetings are events that almost always involve two numbers. One number represents the day of the week; for example, Monday can be thought of as Day 1, Tuesday, Day 2, and so on. The other number represents the time of day, for example 3:00 P.M. Converting these two numbers (day and time) into concrete number images allows us to create pictures and stories to help us better remember important calendar events.

1. Assign a sequential number to each day of the week.
2. For your event, identify the *day number* (e.g., Day 1) and the *time of day* number.
3. Convert these two numbers into concrete images, using either the picture or rhyming association codes. (See Chapter Six.)
4. Link these images together in a wacky picture or story.

Example One

Alison is meeting with her new personal trainer on Monday at 8:00 A.M. To remember this appointment, she uses the memory process outlined above. First she assigns a number to each day of the week, such that Sunday is Day 1 and Saturday is Day 7. The two numbers that now represent her training session are *2* (day of the week) and *8* (session time). Next she converts these numbers into the concrete images they look like, using the picture association code below. This gives her the images of a *swan* (2) and a *snowman* (8). She links the images together to create this wacky story: *A swan (2) waits for a frozen snowman (8) to melt in the sun, so it will have a little pond in which to swim.*

Number	Image	Number	Image
1	Candle		
2	Swan	7	Diving Board
3	Wave	8	Snowman
4	Sailboat	9	Balloon on String
5	Diver	10	Bat and Ball

Example Two

Isabelle creates the following images, using the picture association code, to help her remember her most important business meetings of the week. She substitutes the numbers one through five for the weekdays Monday through Friday. Here is an abbreviated version of her pictorial calendar. Each morning she reviews the day's calendar pictures.

Day	Meeting Time	Numbers & Images	Pictures
Day One (Monday)	3:00 PM	1 (candle), 3 (wave)	A white **candle** floating on a sea green **wave**.
Day Two (Tuesday)	9:00 AM	2 (swan), 9 (balloon)	A black **swan** riding in a red hot air **balloon**.

Exercise One

Turn each of the following meetings into a wacky picture or story by converting the days and meeting times into numbers, and converting the numbers into images. Select either the picture or rhyming association code to convert the numbers into concrete images. Link the images together in a colorful picture or story. Substitute the numbers 1 through 5 for the weekdays Monday through Friday. Weave the information in italics into your calendar picture or story. The first item has been completed for you.

1. *Dentist* appointment on Friday at 2:00 PM

2. *Bridge* club Wednesday at 7:00 PM

3. Interview with *Oprah Winfrey* show on Monday at 4:00 PM

4. School *P.T.A.* meeting at 7:30 PM on Tuesday night

5. *Golf* league at 8:00 on Thursday

Day	Meeting Time	Numbers	Images	Picture/Story
1	2:00 PM	1, 2	Dentist, Candle, Swan	Your Dentist uses a candle to see into the swan's "mouth"
___	_____	_____	_____	_____
				_____
___	_____	_____	_____	_____
				_____
___	_____	_____	_____	_____
				_____
___	_____	_____	_____	_____
				_____

Exercise Two

Select three important calendar events you have this week. Follow the process in Exercise One to create a memorable calendar picture or story for the event.

Day	Meeting Time	Numbers	Images	Picture/Story
___	_____	_____	_____	_____
				_____
___	_____	_____	_____	_____
				_____
___	_____	_____	_____	_____
				_____

Day Four: Environmental Prompts

Skills: Active Observation, Visualization, and Linking
Number of Exercises: Two

Special personal events like birthdays and anniversaries occur in the same calendar month and season each year. Each month and each season has its own recurring environmental prompts. For example, it is hard not to notice the month of October with its many environmental prompts. There are signs of October everywhere in the brightly colored falling leaves, the pumpkins on the doorsteps, and the Halloween decorations in the store windows. If you have a special event that occurs every year in October, you can use pumpkins on doorsteps every year for your memory trigger. Combining environmental prompts with memory skills is a fun and effective way to secure these special events in your memory.

- Actively observe the naturally occurring environmental prompts for each calendar month.
- Select a fixed environmental prompt for each calendar month to serve as a memory hook.
- Create a vivid mental image of the environmental prompt.
- Create a vivid mental image of the special event. Link the image of the environmental prompt and the image of the special event together in a colorful picture or story.

Example One

Bonnie's mother is very sentimental about her birthday, which occurs in the month of October. Her mother especially loves her birthstone, an opal. Anything with opals makes a great birthday present. Every October when Bonnie sees pumpkins on doorsteps, she visualizes them with shining opal eyes. Now pumpkins with opal eyes are her annual memory trigger for her mom's birthday.

Example Two

Jeffrey's dad's birthday is in September. September is back-to-school time in his region of the country. Jeff's dad loves to read and learn new things. Each September, when Jeff sees the kids heading back to school, he visualizes his dad boarding a yellow school bus with a new book under his arm. By linking back-to-school images with his dad's birthday, Jeff has an environmental prompt to help recall his dad's birthday.

Exercise One

For each calendar month below, list as many seasonal prompts as come to mind. Then circle the prompts that have high visibility or special meaning for you. A few examples have been provided to get you started.

Month	Environmental Prompts
January	*New Year's Day*
February	*Valentine's Day*
March	_____
	_____
April	_____
	_____
May	_____
	_____
June	_____
	_____
July	_____
	_____
August	_____
	_____
September	_____
	_____
October	_____
	_____
November	_____
	_____
December	_____
	_____

Exercise Two

Select four special occasions in your life that recur annually. In Column A, write the name of the special occasion. In Column B, write the month in which the special occasion occurs. In Column C, select an environmental prompt to represent the month. In Column D, create a picture or story that links the image of the special occasion with the image of the environmental prompt.

A. Occasion	B. Month	C. Prompt	D. Picture/Story
1. _____	_____	_____	_____
_____	_____	_____	_____
2. _____	_____	_____	_____
_____	_____	_____	_____
3. _____	_____	_____	_____
_____	_____	_____	_____
4. _____	_____	_____	_____
_____	_____	_____	_____

Day Five: Date Links

Skill: Visualization
Number of Exercises: Two

Calendar environmental prompts help trigger recall of special event months, but they do nothing to ensure we will remember the actual date in the month. Using pumpkins to remember that your mom's birthday occurs in October is helpful, but it doesn't guarantee you will remember to call her on the actual date of her birthday. If we are going to remember both the month and the date, we will need a way to weave number images into our existing calendar picture or story.

Example One

Bonnie's mom's birthday is October 21. Earlier she created a picture of an orange pumpkin with opal eyes to help her remember her mom's birthday is in the month of October. Now she wants to weave the date into her picture. Using the picture association code, she substitutes the image of a *swan* for the number *2* and the image of a *candle* for the number *1*. She weaves the images of the swan and the candle into her existing picture. Here is the final picture including both month and date memory prompts.

A *swan sits on top of the pumpkin keeping it warm. A glowing candle inside the carved pumpkin makes the opal eyes glitter.*

Example Two

Jeff created an image of his dad on a school bus, reading a new book, to help him remember his dad's birthday falls in the back-to-school month of September. Now he wants to add his dad's actual birth date to his existing calendar picture. His Dad was born on September second. Jeff uses the rhyming association code to convert the number *two* to the rhyming word *blue*. Now he sees his Dad on the school bus, reading a book with a bright blue cover.

Exercise One

In yesterday's workout, you used environmental prompts to create a memorable picture or story of four special occasions in your life which recur annually. Review the pictures or stories you created. Follow the steps below to add the occasion *dates* to your existing pictures or stories.

1. Identify the actual dates of each special occasion.
2. Convert the dates into concrete images using either the picture or rhyming association code.
3. Incorporate these new number images into your existing picture or story.

Occasion	Date	Number Images	Expanded Story
1. _____	_____	_____	_____
			_____
2. _____	_____	_____	_____
			_____
3. _____	_____	_____	_____
			_____
4. _____	_____	_____	_____
			_____

Exercise Two

For some right brain stimulation, using the space below select one of your stories and turn it into a cartoon. The quality of the art doesn't matter. Have fun with it.

Day Six: Calendar Chores

Skills: Linking and Visualization
Number of Exercises: One

We all have certain special chores or tasks we must remember to perform on an annual basis. If we live in a cold climate, oil burners and fireplaces must be serviced and cleaned once a year in the off-season. If we live in a tropical climate, homes must be pressure-washed at least once a year to prevent mold from growing. In most states, car inspections occur every year in the same month. The actual date is often less important than the month or season in which the chores must be performed. A novel way to remember to perform these annual chores in a timely manner is to link them to recurring calendar holidays and events. Store-bought calendars contain a host of preprinted holidays and events. Calendar holidays and events can be national (Independence Day), ethnic (Chinese New Year), historical (President's Day), religious (Easter), commercial (Valentine's Day), and social (Earth Awareness Day). The point is that almost every month and certainly every season has well-publicized calendar holidays and events. We can use these as memory hooks to help us recall the special chores we must perform annually. Here's how it works:

1. Create a list of your special annual chores.
2. Select recurring calendar events to associate with each special chore.
3. Create visual images of the calendar event and the special chore.
4. Link these images together in a colorful picture or story.

Example One

Since her spouse passed away, Darlene must remember to do many of the annual household chores that her husband used to do. One in particular, which seems to slip her mind, is having the oil burner cleaned during the off-season. The best time for her to schedule this appointment is in the summer, when she has time off from her job as an elementary school teacher. To remind herself to get this chore done in the summer, Darlene links the chore (oil burner cleaning) to her favorite summer holiday (Fourth of July). Using visualization and linking, she imagines colorful Fourth of July fireworks bursting forth from her silver oil burner tank. Each year, when she purchases a new calendar, she draws this image on the July calendar page. At the Fourth of July annual fireworks event, she mentally imagines the fireworks being shot out of her silver oil burner. Pretty soon the two images stick together in her mind.

Exercise One

Round One

Identify three special chores that you must perform on an annual basis. For each annual chore, select a memorable calendar event or holiday that falls closest to when you must perform the chore.

Annual Chores   **Calendar Events**

1. _____   _____
2. _____   _____
3. _____   _____

Round Two

Create a vivid image of the chore and the calendar event. Link these images together in a wacky and colorful story or picture.

Chore Image   **Event Image**   **Picture/Story**

1. _____   _____   _____

                        _____

                        _____

2. _____   _____   _____

                        _____

                        _____

3. _____   _____   _____

                        _____

                        _____

Day Seven: Calendar Accessories

Skill: Linking
Number of Exercises: Two

Have you ever thought about being a fashion designer? Well, here is your chance. You can be the creator of your own wearable calendar accessories. You can wear these accessories on your person or on your clothing. They will go everywhere you go and serve as reminders of special occasions and events. For your designs, you can use standard accessories worn in unusual ways. For example, you can wear a ring backwards, or a wristwatch on the opposite arm. You can also attach common objects, like rubber bands and safety pins, to your clothing. If you are truly a creative soul, you might design novel calendar accessories for your friends and family and give them away as gifts. Who knows where this fashion trend may lead? You might even start a business selling wearable calendar accessories.

Example One

Heidi is a busy but organized person. Each year she writes her personal special occasions on her new calendar, which she dutifully hangs on the wall. This way she can see, for instance, that her best friend's birthday is coming up in a few weeks. As soon as she notes that an important occasion is coming, she starts wearing a visible reminder of the occasion. This way she never forgets. Heidi has decided to wear feathers as a reminder of birthdays. Using an attractive pin, she attaches the feather to her blouse, shirt, or sweater. She uses different colored feathers to represent the birthdays of friends versus family. For her friends' birthdays, she pins on blue feathers. For family birthdays, she uses yellow feathers. And for her boyfriend's birthday, she wears a red feather just above her heart.

Example Two

Adam must remember to buy a present for Mother's Day while on his business trip. As a reminder, he will wear the amber cuff links his mother bought him each day with his business attire.

Exercise One

Select common objects (e.g., rubber band, wristwatch, shoelace) you might wear in unusual ways to remind you of the important occasions in your life. Choose different objects to represent different types of occasions. Describe how you will wear each of these calendar accessories. The occasion's list has been started for you. Complete it with your own special occasions.

Occasion	Object	Accessory Description
Birthdays	_____	_____
Anniversaries	_____	_____
Mother's Day	_____	_____
Father's Day	_____	_____

Exercise Two

Imagine that you are starting a new business selling wearable calendar accessories. You have a staff of very talented people, including a fashion designer and a marketing professional. You will be selling your accessories on television, on the Internet, and in specialty magazines. Hallmark is thinking of partnering with you down the road if your business takes off. For each of the special occasions listed below, design a fashionable accessory (such as pins, scarves, and buttons) that can be worn as a reminder of the special occasion. If you enjoy drawing, sketch out your designs.

Occasion	Fashion Accessory
Birthdays	_____
Anniversaries	_____
Baby Showers	_____
Wedding Showers	_____
Weddings	_____
Mother's Day	_____
Father's Day	_____
Valentine's Day	_____

Dr. Brainfit's Advice Column

Dear Dr. Brainfit,

When my grandmother complained of frequent memory problems, one of the first things the doctor did was take a blood test to determine her level of vitamin B12. What is the reason for this?

Morgan from L.A.

Dear Morgan,

Scientific studies have shown a correlation between low levels of vitamin B12 and Alzheimer's disease. It is fairly routine for medical professionals, suspecting Alzheimer's disease, to check levels of vitamin B12.

Vitamin B12 and Memory

A number of research studies, including Dr. David Snowdon's long-term study of aging nuns, have shown that people with Alzheimer's disease commonly have lower blood levels of vitamin B12 than people without the disease.[1] Studies have also shown that people with lower blood levels of vitamin B12 have a significantly increased risk of developing Alzheimer's disease in their lifetimes. One Swedish study, cited on Vanderbilt University's *Health Plus* Web site, tested the memories of 167 older adults who were free of dementia or depression, but were at a greater statistical risk of developing Alzheimer's disease.[2] On the morning of the test, blood was taken to determine the participants' level of B12. Then memory testing was conducted. Participants with normal levels of B12 scored better on their memory tests than those with lower levels of B12. While there is no scientific evidence to suggest that vitamin B12 actually enhances memory, scientists do know that B vitamins, especially B12, folate, and B6, are crucial for normal brain function. It is believed that getting adequate amounts of B12 may

▼

help the brain stay healthy and preserve memory retention as we age. As we get older, however, we lose some of our ability to absorb vitamin B12. Prolonged antacid use and alcoholism contribute to low levels of B12. Common sources of vitamin B12 include meat and dairy products. Green leafy vegetables, lentils, and oranges are also a good source of folate. Vitamin B6 is found in beans, nuts, legumes, eggs, meats, fish, and whole grains. Many cereals are fortified with B vitamins. The Institute of Medicine recommends that adults over age fifty eat foods fortified with B12 and take a vitamin B12 supplement. Ask your doctor or a medical professional if a B12 supplement is right for you.

Chapter Eight

Remembering Where

"Excuse me but I may be lost . . . Can you give me directions to wherever you're going?"
—ANONYMOUS

Lost and Found

Wouldn't it be great if neuroscientists invented a computer chip that could be implanted in our brains to provide directional information, sort of like the navigational system in a car? That way every time we asked a question like "Has anyone seen my car keys?" or "Do you remember how to get to that great Italian restaurant?" the navigational chip would kick in and provide us with the data to help us track down missing objects or get to our destinations. It's exciting to think about, but pure science fiction for now. In the meantime, we'll have to rely on today's tools for getting our directional bearings—like paper road maps, Web searches, and navigational systems. As for misplaced objects, the old-fashioned approach is probably still the most reliable. It sounds something like this: "Honey, have you seen my . . . ?"

Directionally Challenged

Humor is a great antidote for the things that worry us. Seniors, experiencing mental snags, often exchange their favorite memory jokes to relieve the embarrassment and anxiety associated with memory lapses. Here is one of my favorite memory jokes for the directionally challenged:

A dapper-looking super senior is sitting on a bench, weeping. He is approached by a policeman who asks the despondent man, "Why are you crying, sir?" The elderly man responds, "I'm so upset! I have a beautiful, young, sexy wife who adores me waiting at home." The policeman responds, "That doesn't sound like a problem to me." The man looks up, sighs, and says, "I can't remember where I live!"

Memory Tips for Remembering Where

1. Keep a locator log. Write down the location of important documents you use infrequently, like birth certificates, passports, wills, appraisals, and tax returns.
2. Devise home bases and forget-me-not locations.
3. Say out loud where you are putting objects down, especially if you are feeling rushed or distracted.
4. Write directions to important places on index cards. Order the cards alphabetically and keep them in a file box in the glove compartment of your car.
5. Keep a pad and pen in the car for writing down directions.
6. Consider buying a car with a navigational system.
7. Get a compass for your car and stick it on the dashboard.
8. When you drive, pay attention to landmarks to help you remember directions. For example, you might remind yourself to turn left at the red house with the green shutters.
9. To avoid looking down at written directions while driving, try tape recording the directions. Then all you have to do is push the play button.

10. Create picture symbols to represent directions. They are often easier to follow while driving than written directions.
11. Print out directions from Web sites like MapQuest.com.
12. Join AAA. They will provide a written itinerary for you, and you can call them if you get lost.
13. All police departments (local and state) have phone numbers you can call for routine business. In a pinch, they will help you out with directions.
14. Keep a map in the car.
15. When visiting a new city, purchase a minimap that shows the major intersecting streets. Pay attention to how the streets are laid out. In many cities, streets form a recognizable grid pattern. For example, in New York City, streets run east to west and avenues run north and south.

What's the Workout Rationale?

Writing down directions and addresses may still be your best memory tool for **remembering where**. Still, it is helpful to have additional memory hooks and triggers for those instances when pen and paper are not handy. Using the fundamental memory skills ensures we are actively using our brain, which strengthens the brain's own memory mechanisms.

Let's Work Out!

Welcome to the **Remembering Where** fitness station. As a result of your participation in this week's workout, you'll see how memory skills and organizational tools can boost your aptitude for remembering directions and finding misplaced objects.

Weekly Exercise Planner

The following table lays out the *Brainfit* workout for **Remembering Where.** Each day's workout exercises will be preceded by an Exercise

Introduction, which previews the memory skills to be used for the day and provides examples of how the skills will be applied in the exercises.

Day One: Directional Links

Skill: Linking

Number of Exercises: Two

First-letter linking is a fun and easy memory skill for remembering a simple set of directions. Link the first letters of a directional sequence together to form a word (*acronym*). Link the first letters of a directional sequence together to form a sentence (*acrostic*).

Example One

Cathy is a new college student at Boston University, hailing from rural Kentucky. Getting around a city the size of Boston makes her a little nervous. To get from her apartment on Beacon Hill to Boston University at Kenmore Square, Cathy must take the MBTA subway system. The subway stops along the way are Beacon, Arlington, Copley, and Kenmore. To help her remember this sequence, Cathy uses an acrostic. She links the first letters of each stop, in sequence, to create this memorable acrostic sentence: Boston Announces Cathy (from) Kentucky.

Example Two

Miguel stops at a service station and asks for direction to the nearest Wal-Mart store. The attendant quickly rattles off the following directions:

- Left on Congress
- Right on Hypoluxa
- Left on Orange Grove
- Right into Wal-Mart

As Miguel does not have a piece of paper handy, he must quickly commit this simple set of directions to memory. Miguel easily connects the left-right sequence to marching soldiers. To remember the street sequence, he uses first-letter linking. By stringing together the first letters of each street name he comes up with the acronym *CHOW* (Congress, Hypoluxa, Orange Grove, and Wal-Mart). Which, incidentally, reminds him he needs to pick up dog food at Wal-Mart.

Example Three

Jose prefers acronyms to acrostics as a memory tool. However there are many first-letter links that do not easily convert into words. In cases like this, Jose looks for hidden words within random letter groupings. For instance, the first-letter link BST can be stretched a bit to become the word BEST.

Exercise One

Friends have arranged dinner at the Palm Beach Fish Market & Bistro, a new restaurant in West Palm Beach. You are running late. As you pull out of your driveway, you call the restaurant on your cell phone for directions. The hostess tells you to get on Route 95 North and get off at Southern Boulevard heading east. From Southern Boulevard, take Dixie Highway heading north. In your mind, you make a quick note of the essential first-letter links which are SBE (Southern Boulevard East) and DHN (Dixie Highway North).

Use first-letter linking to turn these two letter groupings into memorable acrostics.

First-Letter Links	Acrostic
SBE	_____
DHN	_____

Exercise Two

Below is a list of random letter groupings. Use your imagination to stretch these letter groupings into real words. The first one is done for you.

Random Letters	Words
COFE	*Coffee*
BND	_____
SPT	_____
PLNT	_____
BLCK	_____

Day Two: Rhythm & Rhyme

Skill: Verbalization
Number of Exercises: Two

Have you ever noticed how easy it is to learn the words to a country-and-western song? This is because so many of the words rhyme. An easy way to get simple directions to stick in your memory is to create simple rhymes.

Example One

Wayne's mother is beginning to experience some minor memory confusion with regard to driving directions. When Wayne gives his mother directions these days, he always adds a little memory-boosting rhyme. Just recently, he reminded his mother she needed to take the highway entrance marked *west* to get to her friend Fanny's house in Wellington. He ended his directions by saying, "Remember, Mom, "*West is best.*"

Example Two

Sarah needs to remember that the wedding is being held at the church on Greenbrier. So she makes up this simple rhyme: "The church is on Greenbrier; in attendance will be a friar."

Exercise One

Create simple rhymes to help you remember the following directions and addresses. The word that needs to be rhymed is underlined. The first one is done for you.

Direction

1. *Take the exit marked <u>4B.</u>*

2. Let's meet at the deli on <u>Maken.</u>

Rhyme

Forget 4B, poor me.

_____

_____

_____

3. The diet center is on the corner
   of <u>Heather.</u>

   _____

   _____

4. The veterinarian's office is on <u>Jog.</u>

   _____

   _____

5. The courthouse is two blocks
   down on <u>Long.</u>

   _____

   _____

6. The office supply store is on <u>Draper.</u>

   _____

   _____

Exercise Two

Pick the addresses of five friends' or relatives' homes and make up a simple rhyme that would help a visitor remember the street where they live.

Street Name   **Rhyme**

1. _____   _____

2. _____   _____

3. _____   _____

4. _____   _____

5. _____   _____

Day Three: Picture Perfect

Skill: Visualization
Number of Exercises: Two

Have you ever noticed how many street names and building names contain built-in imagery? You can turn these memory-boosting images into wacky pictures and stories.

- Look for built-in images in directional information.
- Convert street numbers into concrete visual images (see Chapter Six).
- Link images together to form a wacky story or picture.

Example One

Zachary is dropping his dog off at a new kennel on the corner of Jog and Lantana. To remember this address without writing it down, he looks for built-in images in the street names. Jog is easy. He pictures his dog in jogging shoes running toward the kennel. Lantana sounds like banana. He imagines his jogging dog slipping on a banana peel and sliding into the open kennel door.

Example Two

The customer's new warehouse is on Bentmore Avenue. To remember this address, you break Bentmore into two syllables. Using the built-in images in the two syllables, you come up with a picture of the customer in the warehouse *bending* (Bent) down to get *more* (more) product.

Exercise One

Look for built-in images in the following location names. Link these images together to create a silly picture or phrase. The first one is done for you.

Name	Picture or Phrase
The Mayo Clinic	*A hospital which serves nothing but mayonnaise sandwiches.*
The Pembroke Museum	_____

The Sunapee Medical Center _____

Congress Street _____

Corner of Turnbull and Charles _____

Bangor, Maine _____

Manitoba, Canada _____

Exercise Two

Use the picture association code below to help you convert the following street addresses into wacky pictures or phrases. The first one is done for you.

Number	Picture	Number	Picture
0	Egg	6	Rattlesnake
1	Candle	7	Diving Board
2	Swan	8	Snowman
3	Ocean Wave	9	Balloon (on a string)
4	Sailboat	10	Bat & Ball
5	Diver		

Street Address

Picture/Phrase

5 High Street

*A **diver** (5) jumping off the **high** diving board*

22 Haggets Pond _____

43 Richmond Lane _____

1 Seminole Circle _____

9 Weathersfield Avenue _____

Day Four: Leprechauns & Rabbits

Skills: Visualization and Linking
Number of Exercises: Two

Have you ever been given a quick sequence of left-right turns to remember? If you don't write the sequence down, it's easy to get confused. To boost your memory for these common directional signals, try substituting concrete images for the words left and right.

Left Turn = Leprechaun
Right Turn = Rabbit

Weave the left and right turn images into a wacky story or picture.

Example One

The policeman tells Ethan, "Proceed two blocks and take your first right." To boost her memory, she visualizes two Lego blocks one on top of the other with a rabbit (*right turn*) sitting on top, dressed like a traffic cop.

Example Two

The gas station attendant tells Jonah to take a right turn after the railroad tracks, and then follow the signs for the Florida Turnpike. Jonah creates two quick images to capture the directions in memory. His first image is a rabbit (*right turn*) riding on a commuter train and his second image is a palm tree lying on the railroad tracks (*Florida Turnpike*).

Example Three

The hotel concierge gives Brandon directions to the nearest bank. He tells Brandon to exit the hotel and turn left, and at the first intersection, take a right. The bank is on the left side of the street. Brandon turns the directional information into three snapshots: 1) a leprechaun dressed like a bellboy outside the hotel, 2) a rabbit directing traffic at the intersection, and 3) a leprechaun dressed as a security guard outside the bank.

Exercise One

Turn the following sets of directions into wacky pictures or stories. Assign fixed association images to the words left and right (e.g., left turn = leprechaun, right turn = rabbit). Substitute other fixed images for common directional signals (e.g., city block = Lego block). Briefly describe your pictures and stories under each set of directions.

1. Turn left at the Dunkin' Donuts, proceed to the next traffic light, and bear right onto Peach Tree road.

_____

_____

_____

_____

2. Cross over the Washington Memorial Bridge, proceed to Exit 10, bear left off the exit.

_____

_____

_____

_____

3. Follow the Yellowstone River until you come to a fork in the road. At the fork, turn right and proceed to the campgrounds.

_____

_____

_____

_____

4. Get off at Sunset Boulevard East, and then proceed four blocks to the police station, which will be on the left side of the street.

_____

_____

_____

_____

Exercise Two

Select one of the sets of directions above. Create a cartoon picture instead of words to capture the images you've created. Drawing is a right brain activity. Forming verbal sentences is a left brain activity.

Day Five: Alliteration

Skills: Verbalization and Linking
Number of Exercises: One

Another way to remember directions involving left-right sequences is to substitute words beginning with the letter *L* for left turns and words beginning with the letter *R* for right turns. Your *L* and *R* words can then be linked together to form fun and memorable sentences. These sentences will capitalize on the memory power of alliteration. Alliteration is the repetition of the same sounds at the beginning of words.

Example One

Rosa asks the parking lot attendant at the mall for directions to the highway. The attendant responds with an abrupt, "Left out of the lot, left at the light, your first right is the highway entrance." Since there is a line of cars behind her, Rosa does not ask the attendant to repeat the sequence. Instead she quickly turns the left-left-right sequence into the following simple sentence: "Lucy loves roses."

Example Two

Sharon arrives late at night at the airport and rents a car. As she is exiting the rental car lot, she notices that her gas tank is not full. Not knowing exactly how far she needs to travel to get to her hotel, she decides to fill up now and report this oversight later to the rental car company. As she exits the rental car lot, she asks the attendant for directions to the nearest gas station. He responds with, "Take a right out of the lot, at the first traffic light take a left onto Bank Street, the gas station will be about one block up on your left." Sharon notes the easy sequence of right, left, left, and quickly forms the memory sentence, "Rita likes lasagna."

Exercise One

Below is a sequence of directional signals. See how quickly you can turn each set of directional signals into simple word sentences. Use words that begin with the letter *L* for left-hand turns, and words that begin with the letter *R* for right-hand turns. Challenge a friend. See who is fastest at converting the turning signals into sentences.

Signals

Sentences

Left, Right, Left, Right

Left, Left, Right, Right

Right, Left, Right, Left

Right, Right, Left, Left

Right, Left, Left, Right

Left, Right, Right, Left

Left, Right, Left, Left

Right, Left, Right, Right

Day Six: Mix & Match
Skills: Visualization, Verbalization, and Linking
Number of Exercises: One

As you become more adept at using the memory skills, you will find yourself naturally mixing and matching the skills without even realizing it. In the following exercise workout, you'll experiment with freely combining the memory skills to remember important locations.

Example One

Tanya needs to remember her car is parked in the South Lot, Section B, Row 12 of the public beach parking lot. First she creates an abbreviation of the critical location information, which she denotes as SB12. Then she substitutes word images for each letter and number. Moving from left to right her word substitution is *sunny (S)*, *beach (B)*, at *noon (12)*.

Example Two

John needs to remember his rental license plate so he will be able to locate his car tomorrow morning in the hotel parking lot. His license plate number is BST 008. To remember his license plate he stretches BST into the word *Best*. Then he converts the numbers into the images they look like. He sees two snowballs (00), one on top of the other forming a snowman (8). He imagines he has just won the *Best Snowman* contest.

Exercise One

Mix and match the fundamental memory skills to help you remember the following locations. Experiment with your favorite memory techniques for remembering where. Key information to be remembered is underlined.

1. Your doctor's office is in <u>Pod B</u> next to the <u>water cooler</u>.

   _____

   _____

2. Your car is parked at the mall in the <u>North Lot</u>, Row <u>F9</u>.

_____

_____

3. Your friend is in hospital room <u>24A</u> in the <u>Blue Wing</u>.

_____

_____

4. The children's department is on <u>Level 3</u> next to <u>housewares</u>.

_____

_____

5. You've hidden the birthday <u>present</u> in your <u>closet</u> under the <u>hatbox</u>.

_____

_____

6. The conference is being held in <u>Room C</u> across from the <u>mailroom</u>.

_____

_____

7. The wedding is in the <u>Grand Ballroom</u> on the <u>Mezzanine Level</u>.

_____

_____

8. Your grandmother just moved to the <u>Rocky Mount</u> Assisted Living Home on <u>Shrewsbury</u> Street.

_____

_____

9. The meeting is across town in the <u>Four Seasons Hotel</u>.

_____

_____

Day Seven: Lost & Found

Skills: Active Observation, Visualization, and Verbalization
Number of Exercises: Two

When it comes to remembering where, there is nothing more aggravating than trying to locate the things we ourselves misplace. So what is the solution? Dr. Samuel Johnson once said, ". . . The true art of memory is the art of attention." We misplace items, not because our brain is aging, but because we don't pay attention to where we put things down. We don't pay attention because we are rushing, distracted, or multitasking. So how do we put a stop to this frustrating, time-wasting phenomenon? The answer is basic. Pay attention and get organized!

- Use all five senses to pay attention to where you put important objects. (*See* yourself put the keys down on the counter. *Hear* the clink of keys as they hit the counter.)
- Take a mental snapshot of yourself in the act of putting items down.
- Tell yourself and others, out loud, where you are putting things.
- Get organized. Apply the golden rule of organization: "A place for everything and everything in its place."

Example One

Barry is always forgetting his car keys in his golf bag. Often he gets to his car after a round of golf, only to realize he doesn't have his keys. By the time he gets back to the club-house, his bag has been stored and he has to ask one of the bag boys to pull his bag out of storage so he can get his keys. The last time this happened, he heard the bag boys taking bets on how long it would take before he was back looking for his keys. That was the last straw for Barry. Now every time he puts his keys in his golf bag, he stops and focuses. He takes a mental picture of himself putting the keys in the bag. He tells his partner, "Hey, remind me I put my keys in the bag." To further prompt his memory, he draws a picture of a set of keys on his score card. Pretty soon remembering the car keys is automatic.

Example Two

Carla is a working single mom. She shares her car with her three teenage sons. It seems like everyone in her household is always rushing off somewhere . . . to work, to basketball practice, to after-school jobs. Car keys are easily misplaced. When keys go missing, the blame game begins with everyone pointing a finger at everyone else. Carla decides to remedy this situation. She attaches a metal hook to the wall near the garage door. All keys must be retrieved and returned to this location. When someone forgets to put the keys on the hook, the perpetrator must put five dollars into a forget-me-not kitty. At the end of the month, the money goes to the person with the best record for not forgetting to put the car keys on the hook.

Exercise One

One approach for reducing the number of times items go missing is to devise a home base for each item you frequently misplace. If an item is used inside and outside your home, it's wise to create both a "home" and an "away" base. If an item is used upstairs and downstairs, it makes sense to designate both an upstairs and a downstairs home base. You'll want to avoid home bases like shirt pockets, where items can easily fall out, or get tossed into the wash.

In addition to the items here, select three to five items you frequently misplace at home and at work. For each selected item, devise a "home base" location. For the next week, use these home base locations religiously. Keep track of how many times you misplace one of the items. Keep repeating the process, until your misplaced item score for a single week is zero.

Items	Home Base
Car keys	Keyhook or console by the front door
Wallet or purse	_____
Glasses	_____
Cell Phone	_____
_____	_____
_____	_____
_____	_____

Dr. Brainfit's Advice Column

Dear Dr. Brainfit,

I have a very spiritual friend who believes that meditation alters the mind in ways that lead to heightened consciousness. Is there any scientific evidence for this?

Lou from Minneapolis

Dear Lou,

Scientists know that external stimuli, like playing bridge, can stimulate healthy brain changes. Some scientists are starting to explore how internal mental stimuli, like meditation, can rewire the brain in positive ways, too.

Meditation and Brain Changes

The scientific term for the brain's ability to change its structure and function is called **neuroplasticity.** (See the appendix for more information on neuroplasticity.) This dynamic ability of the brain to change can now be observed through the use of highly advanced imaging technology. We can see that when the brain is engaged and stimulated, neural connectors, called dendrites, expand and strengthen. Conversely, neural connectors that are rarely used shrink and weaken. Until recently, neuroscience looked only at how the brain changes in response to external stimuli. Recently, however, neuroscientist Richard Davidson of the University of Wisconsin at Madison, conducted a research study with Buddhist monks in Dharamsala, India, to see whether the brain can change in response to purely internal mental signals. The results of the study are summarized by Sharon Begley in *Science Journal*, November 2004.[1]

Initial results suggest that the brain is altered as a result of dedicated, long-term meditation. In the study conducted by Dr. Davidson, experienced monks

▼

▼

who had spent more than ten thousand hours in meditation showed a significant increase in a high-frequency brain activity, called gamma waves, during compassion meditation. Novice monks engaged in compassion meditation showed only a slight increase in gamma activity, suggesting that the brains of the experienced monks had been altered through years of meditation. Additionally, activity in the left prefrontal cortex of the experienced monks (the site of positive emotions), greatly exceeded activity in the right prefrontal cortex (the site of negative emotions and anxiety). In her article in *Science Journal*, Sharon Begley concludes that this study "... opens up the tantalizing possibility that the brain, like the rest of the body, can be altered intentionally. Just as aerobics sculpt the muscles, so mental training sculpts the gray matter in ways scientists are only beginning to fathom."

Chapter Nine

Mental Agility Challenges for the Left Brain

"Think of the brain as a work in progress that continues from birth until the day you die. At every moment, your activities and thoughts are modifying your brain."
—RICHARD RESTAK, M.D., *MOZART'S BRAIN AND THE FIGHTER PILOT*

Cognitive Changes as We Age

Cognition refers to the higher mental processes of perceiving, remembering, and thinking. One of the best ways to assess cognitive change as we age is through longitudinal studies like K. Warner Schaie's *Developmental Influences on Adult Intelligence: The Seattle Longitudinal Study.*[1] In this famous study, a population of five thousand people is being studied over the course of their lifetimes for changes in cognitive abilities. Starting in 1956 individuals in the study are retested every seven years in the cognitive areas of verbal meaning (recognizing and comprehending words), spatial ability (mentally rotating objects in space), reasoning (identifying regularities and principles of rules), number skills (arithmetic computation), and word fluency (recalling words that fit into categories, such as names of birds).

Dr. Schaie found that deficits in the cognitive abilities across all measures were not seen before age sixty, and by age seventy-four only a small decline was observed. Surprisingly, by age eighty-one cognitive abilities still remained strong for the majority of the population. Fewer than half the people in the study showed declines from the previous testing period. Dr. Schaie also looked at the question of whether cognitive decline with age can be reversed through an "educational" program. He found that two-thirds of the people who participated in an educational program that included occasional booster sessions showed significant improvement, and 40 percent returned to pre-decline cognitive performance levels, with these positive effects being maintained even after seven years.

Changes in Mental Agility

Mental agility, a subset of cognitive ability, is most affected by the normal aging process. Changes in mental agility can be seen in the areas of:

- Grasping and solving problems quickly
- Holding several items at once in short-term memory
- Switching rapidly from one context to another context
- Recalling names, events, and facts quickly
- Seeing the big picture quickly without having to plow through all the details
- Thinking on one's feet

A common denominator in this list is the ability to process information quickly. The most common and "normal" mental deficit as we age is the slowing down of the speed of processing information. It is not that our cognitive abilities are lost to us as we age, it just takes longer to get the wheels cranking.

On the bright side, the brain is a dynamic organ (see Dr. F. M. Crinella's article on "Learning, Memory, and Neural Plasticity" in the appendix) with a great capacity to adapt, rewire, and compensate in the face of normal mental aging. Neurons respond to mental stimulation and an intellectually enriched environment in ways that appear to moderate and, in many instances, overcome the physical changes associated with brain aging. "Use it or lose it" appears to be our best avenue of defense when it comes to preserving and boosting mental agility. To fully use your brain, you will want to engage in mental exercises and activities that target the whole brain.

Cross-Train Your Brain

What does a robust mental agility program look like? If you go to a personal fitness trainer or participate in circuit training programs, your physical fitness regimen will involve cross-training. You will alternate between aerobic exercises that get your heart rate up and promote cardiovascular health (think treadmill), and a strength building program to build muscle mass (think free weights and Nautilus equipment). The cerebral cortex of the brain, with its two hemispheres, makes it naturally adaptive to brain fitness cross-training. The best mental agility programs will target both the left and right hemispheres of the brain. It is generally agreed that the different hemispheres of the brain are responsible for different modes of thinking. Exercise programs that address multiple modes of thinking are more enriching and stimulating than exercise programs that focus on only one mode of thinking. According to Dr. Richard Restak (*Mozart's Brain and the Fighter Pilot*) "the brain operates most efficiently when different rather than the same areas are activated simultaneously.[2] Engaging in two same brain activities like reading and listening to the news is virtually impossible. However, reading and listening to classical music works well together."

The chart below summarizes the different modes of thinking between the left and right hemispheres of the brain.

Left Brain Thinking Processes	Right Brain Thinking Processes
Logical	Holistic
Analytical	Intuitive
Quantitative	Synthesizing
Planned/Structured	Fluid/Spontaneous
Fact-based	Feeling-based
Sequential Processing	Simultaneous Processing
Verbal	Visual-Spatial

Tips for Left Brain Stimulation

1. Play word games like Boggle and Scrabble.

2. Alternate your pleasure reading selections between book genres (e.g. poetry, novels, nonfiction, mystery, memoirs, science fiction, plays).

3. Learn or relearn a foreign language.

4. Write your memoirs.

5. Keep a travel journal of your vacation trips.

6. Plan and organize a fabulous dream vacation with all details included.

7. Do the verbal brainteasers in the local papers.

8. Do crossword puzzles. If you are a beginner, get the easy workbooks with the answers in the back.

9. Select a controversial news story that interests you. Gather all the facts you can about the issue from reading and watching TV. Put the pertinent facts on index cards. Then analyze the facts and draw your own conclusion. Current topics you might analyze include:

   - Is the war in Iraq justified?

   - Should we have socialized health care?

   - Is the United States safe from terrorist attacks?

   - Should we continue to fund the space program?

10. Play card games like bridge, gin rummy, and poker.

11. Play games that involve strategy and logic, like chess.

12. Research an interesting or controversial topic on the Internet.

13. Learn a new software application.

14. Find fun, left brain games to play, using the library, bookstores, and toy stores.

15. Invent your own word games to challenge your friends. Use the models in this chapter to construct your games.

What's the Workout Rationale?

This week's workout will focus on fun, left brain activities associated with verbal reasoning and logic. Next week's workout will focus on right brain activities associated with visual-spatial patterns and reasoning. Over the next two weeks, you will cross-train your brain for maximum whole brain fitness.

Let's Work Out!

Let's start cross-training your brain. As you begin your mental aerobic workout, here are some things to keep in mind. First, you may feel a little tired after a brain workout. This is because mental exercise, like physical exercise, requires energy. When you work out mentally, brain cells start communicating with each other, and when this happens blood flow increases to the brain, bringing with it oxygen and glucose. Second, avoid frustration by starting slowly and pacing yourself. You wouldn't begin lifting fifty-pound weights until you could comfortably lift five-pound weights. Do not feel like you have to complete all the exercises for a particular day. If you are feeling tired or anxious, take a break. If you are having fun, keep going. Third, the goal of a mental agility program is to find interesting and varied ways to play with your brain, not strain your brain. Waking up your brain and having fun are perfectly compatible.

Weekly Exercise Planner

This week's mental agility workout is exercise rich. This means there may be more exercises than fit into a ten-minute workout session. Each day, experiment with the different types of exercises, but do not feel like you have to complete all the items in a particular exercise. Also, consider spreading out the daily exercises over the course of the day, rather than completing them in one sitting. For instance, you may choose to invest ten minutes in the morning and ten minutes in the evening. The solutions for this week's exercises can be found at the end of the chapter.

Mental Agility Challenges for the Left Brain

Day One: Homonyms & Synonyms
Skills: Left Brain
Number of Exercises: Two

Today you will engage in two verbal agility exercises. In the first exercise you will be asked to find pairs of homonyms. In the second, you will be asked to find pairs of synonyms. Before you begin, read the definitions of homonyms and synonyms below and review the examples.

Homonyms Defined

Homonyms are fun, no matter where they pop up. They're fun in riddles (there's a rabbit grower who combs his hare every morning). They are also great in puzzles. In order to be classified as homonyms, two words must sound exactly or very nearly the same but have different meanings and spellings. Using this rule, *hare* and *hair* are homonyms, but *hare* and *here* are not. In the examples that follow, the idea is to find the two missing words that make a sensible sentence. The two missing words are homonyms.

Example One

Sentence: It is a _____ idea to try to _____ yourself a glass of milk with your eyes closed.

Answer: *poor* and *pour*

Example Two

Sentence: They left _____ books over _____, under the tree.
Solution: *their* and *there*

Synonyms Defined

Synonyms are words that have the same or almost the same meaning. For example, *Rock* and *stone* are synonyms. *Rock* and *solid mass* are not synonyms.

Example One

Which word is not a synonym of the others?
tired, weary, fatigued, exhausted, resting
Answer: *resting*

Exercise One: Homonyms

Okay, now it's time for you to find the pairs of homonyms that make these sentences sensible.

1. If it starts to _____, let's _____ in the horses.
2. The auto mechanic stubbed his _____ on a _____ truck.
3. _____ careful not to get a _____ sting.
4. There's _____ way my little brother would _____ the answer to this question.
5. The rams looked like they would _____ horns, _____ then they walked away from each other.
6. Keeping your _____ warm when you ice skate can be quite a _____.
7. The judge said, "Will the defendants _____ enter their _____."
8. The chef had a _____ ability to _____ a carrot in fifteen seconds.
9. The actor decided to take his _____ in front of the _____ of a tree.
10. The temperamental cow only _____ when she was in a good _____.
11. You don't need _____ pieces of bread _____ make an open-faced sandwich.
12. The _____ was renting a room in a house less than a mile from the Canadian _____.
13. Some _____ I feel like I'm walking around in a _____.
14. I can always count on my aunt to _____ me a present every time she stops _____ for a visit.
15. The itching _____ be caused by a flea, a tick, or a _____.
16. The sailor _____ up his boat during high _____.
17. A smart dog _____ from any areas where _____ hang out.
18. After a half-hour _____, the nurse measured my height and _____.
19. A defective _____ could _____ and my bicycle would fail to stop.
20. It's a _____ in the neck to clean thick soot off the window _____.
21. The _____ problem in grooming a lion is combing out its _____.
22. My throat became _____ after the _____ and buggy ride.
23. Many of the prospectors who _____ gold didn't _____ the harsh working conditions.
24. I've never known a _____ to put _____ in its hair.
25. _____ people can figure out the _____ of a whole bunch of numbers in their heads.

Exercise Two: Synonyms
Circle the word in each group that is not a synonym of the others.

1. barren
   bare
   empty
   bleak
   desolate

2. kind
   benevolent
   charitable
   empathetic
   gentle

3. creative
   fanciful
   imaginative
   constructive
   inventive

4. frigid
   winter
   frosty
   glacial
   frozen

5. rambunctious
   boisterous
   unruly
   disorderly
   troublesome

6. panic
   terror
   violent
   fear
   anxiety

7. astute
   sharp
   clever
   thoughtful
   shrewd

8. dashing
   dapper
   neat
   jaunty
   natty

9. stormy
   tempestuous
   raging
   blustery
   angry

10. blend
    mix
    intermingle
    fuse
    combine

Day Two: Word Scrambles

Skills: Left Brain
Number of Exercises: Two

Many verbal brainteasers involve unscrambling scrambled words. Words can be scrambled in many different formats. In today's exercises you'll work with circular and categorical word scrambles. These word scrambles will challenge both your verbal and visual-spatial skills.

Example One: Circular Scrambles

We read English words left to right. We know where the first letter is and in which direction we read. Circular words are trickier. The first letter can be anywhere in the circle and we don't know if we read it clockwise or counterclockwise. In the example below, find the word hidden in the circle.

Solution: If you start with the letter P and go clockwise, you see the word *pencil*.

Example Two: Categorical Scrambles

In this type of word scramble, you need to find the word that is not of the same category as the other words. The category provides the clue to unscrambling the words. The more familiar you are with a particular category type, the easier it will be to recall and unscramble these category-specific words. In the following example, find the word that does not fit the category *Tree*.

Unscramble the letters to find the word that does not fit the category *Tree*.

a. ralpop

b ceheb

c malpe

d. doowgod

e. syorfthisa

Answer: a. poplar (tree), b. beech (tree), c. maple (tree), d. dogwood (tree), e. forsythia (bush)

Exercise One: Circular Scrambles

Sharpen your eyes and see if you can find the words hidden in the circles. The first letter of the word can occur at any point in the circle. Check your answers at the end of the chapter.

1. E
    N   D
    V   E
      I
Answer:

5. R
    A   E
    S   R
      E
Answer:

9. C
    N   H
    U   C
      R
Answer:

2. E
    K   N
    O   B
      R
Answer:

6. S
    E   O
    H   O
      T
Answer:

10. L
    E   E
    M   T
      O
Answer:

3. O
    D   I
    I   E
      N
Answer:

7. I
    V   O
    N   L
      I
Answer:

11. H
    R   Y
    M   T
      H
Answer:

4. P
    L   O
    E   E
      P
Answer:

8. Z
    E   A
    A   L
      B
Answer:

12. I
    E   L
    G   A
      O
Answer:

Exercise Two: Categorical Scrambles

Unscramble the letters to find the word that does not belong to the category. Circle the word that does not fit. Check your answers at the end of the chapter.

1. Breeds of dogs
   a. naipels
   b. herdseph
   c. gleabe
   d karsh
   e. rierret

2. Types of flowers
   a. rigoldma
   b. letrut
   c. lutip
   d. peniatu
   e. liovet

3. Types of birds
   a. geonip
   b reysop
   c. cocapek
   d. nuteap
   e. parsrow

4. Names of oceans
   a. tictalna
   b. niadin
   c. rictac
   d. revri
   e. ficacip

5. Names of languages
   a. centac
   b. shilgen
   c. webher
   e. schinee
   f. hawsili

213

Day Three: Word Search

Skills: Left Brain

Number of Exercises: Two

Exercise One

To solve this word puzzle, start with the first clue, which leads to a four-letter word. For the second clue, add the given letter to the previous word. Using the given clue, rearrange the letters to form a word that completes the second row of the puzzle. Continue this process until you have completed all four rows of the puzzle. Check your answers at the end of the chapter.

Japanese Wine

Hockey Equipment (+T)

Red Riding Hood's Prop (+B)

A Hurdle to Overcome (+C)

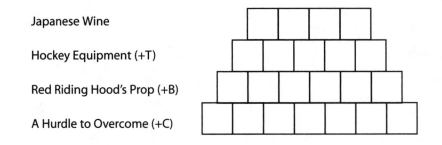

Exercise Two

The names of thirty-two birds can be found vertically, horizontally, and diagonally in the grid. Twenty-one letters are not used; when these letters are read row by row, they spell the names of two more birds. What are they? Write down your answer.

N	I	P	E	L	I	C	A	N	C	N
G	A	E	B	L	E	L	G	A	E	R
H	R	N	I	D	M	R	N	T	I	E
N	R	A	R	G	O	A	T	A	L	T
E	U	R	D	K	R	V	C	S	I	U
Q	B	C	O	Y	N	E	E	A	E	R
G	A	C	F	D	F	N	H	A	W	K
I	K	O	P	E	N	G	U	I	N	E
A	O	C	A	S	S	O	W	A	R	Y
L	O	K	R	O	B	L	C	R	S	B
B	K	A	A	O	U	D	A	H	E	U
A	O	T	D	G	Z	F	R	N	R	N
T	O	I	I	I	Z	I	D	O	U	T
R	R	E	S	W	A	N	I	C	T	I
O	E	L	E	I	R	C	N	L	L	N
S	T	O	R	K	D	H	A	A	U	G
S	O	G	N	I	M	A	L	F	V	R

ALBATROSS   HAWK
BIRD OF PARADISE   KESTREL
BUNTING   KIWI
BUZZARD   KOOKABURRA
CANARY   MACAW
CARDINAL   PELICAN
CASSOWARY   PENGUIN
COCKATIEL   QUAIL
CONDOR   RAVEN
CRANE   ROOK
DOVE   STORK
EAGLE   SWAN
FALCON   TERN
FLAMINGO   TURKEY
GOLDFINCH   VULTURE
GOOSE   WREN

Day Four: Things in Common

Skills: Left Brain
Number of Exercises: Three

Today, your mental agility workout includes three different exercises. Your goal in each exercise, however, will be the same: to determine what the items have *in common*. The following examples are for Exercise One only.

Example One

In Exercise One, you will be presented with two columns of lists. Your goal is to find what is common to all the items in Column A that also makes them different from the items in Column B.

Column A	Column B
Rhode Island	Maine
New York	Kentucky
North Carolina	Oregon
South Dakota	Georgia
West Virginia	Illinois

Answer: Items in Column A are two words.

Example Two

Column A	Column B
White House	Empire State Building
Capitol Building	Disneyland
Lincoln Memorial	Liberty Bell
Smithsonian Institution	Grand Canyon
Library of Congress	Mount Rushmore

Answer: Items in Column A are tourist attractions in Washington, D.C.

Example Three

Column A	Column B
Cope	Piglet
Kept	Tall
Graph	Flag
Type	Open
Happy	Ship

Answer: Words in Column A all have a "p" as the second-to-last letter.

Exercise One

Find what is common to all the items in Column A that also makes them different from the items in Column B.

1.

Column A	Column B
Giggle	Swan
Peeled	Happiness
Passes	Clock
Puppy	Referee
Carrier	Lunch

Answer:

2.

Column A	Column B
Super	Knot
Bat	Freight
Spider	Product
Handy	Bounty
Fire	Hello

Answer:

3.

Column A	Column B
Life	Gather
Money	Study
People	Knowing
Wired	Read
MAD	Look

Answer:

4.

Column A	Column B
Brett Favre	Tyrell Davis
Drew Bledsoe	Jerry Rice
Randall Cunningham	Sammy Sosa
Troy Aikman	Mike Ditka
Kordell Stewart	Pete Sampras

Answer:

5.	Column A	Column B
	13	8
	19	18
	23	21
	31	25
	37	32

Answer:

6.	Column A	Column B
	Cicada	Piranha
	Praying Mantis	Orangutan
	Beetle	Aardvark
	Flea	Shank
	Cockroach	Python

Answer:

7.	Column A	Column B
	Moment	Yard
	Jiffy	Ton
	Instant	Calorie
	Second	Carat
	Decade	Decibel

Answer:

8.	Column A	Column B
	Charles Schulz	Ernest Hemingway
	Scott Adams	Edgar Allen Poe
	Cathy Guisewite	David Copperfield
	Gary Larson	George Elliot
	Garry Trudeau	Charles Dickens

Answer:

9.	Column A	Column B
	Linguini	Spumoni
	Macaroni	Zucchini
	Manicotti	Pepperoni
	Rigatoni	Salami
	Vermicelli	Cappuccino

Answer:

10.	Column A	Column B
	Sing	It's A Small World
	Bein' Green	London Bridge
	"C" Is For Cookie	Do Re Mi
	Five People	Hokey Pokey
	In My Family	Somewhere over
	Rubber Duckie	the Rainbow

Answer:

11.	**Column A**	**Column B**	12.	**Column A**	**Column B**
	Outback	Path		Pepper	Salt
	Walkabout	Hike		Seuss	Magician
	Joey	Climb		Spock	Leprechaun
	Tucker	Tent		Jekyll	Witch
	Boomerang	Canoe		Doolittle	Warlock

Answer: Answer:

Exercise Two

What do the following words have in common?

HOT	OFF	POWDER
ROYAL	JET	LIME
STEEL		FLAME

Answer:

Exercise Three

Look at how the objects in the boxes might be linked together. Find as many ways as you can to pair the objects. Some pairs are obvious, while others are more subtle. Each picture may be paired with at least two other pictures. There is no single right answer.

How many pairs did you make?

Day Five: Sequence Solving

Skills: Left Brain

Number of Exercises: One

Some things in life have a sequence. There's a rule that puts things in order and leads to the next item.

Example One

Find the rule that gives meaning to the sequence. Use the rule to find the next item in the sequence.

1,   3,   5,   7,   9,   11,   _____

Answer: Yes, the next number in this sequence is 13. There's more than one way to see the rule. For instance, you may have seen it as odd numbers or numbers that start with 1 and keep increasing by 2.

Example Two

Use the rule to find the next item in this sequence.

Pluto, Neptune, Uranus, Saturn, Jupiter, _____

Answer: That's right; the answer is Mars. The rule is the names of the planets in reverse order.

Exercise One

Identify the rule and then use it to find the next item in the sequences below.

1. Bush, Clinton, Bush, Reagan, Carter, Ford, Nixon, _____

2. 11, 14, 17, 20, 23, _____

3. c, f, h, k, m, p,_____

4. 12:00, 12:50, 1:40, 2:30, 3:20, 4:10, 5:00, _____

5. Wyoming, Wisconsin, West Virginia, Washington, Virginia, _____

6. 3, 6, 12, 24, 48, _____

7. Martin Luther King Day, Presidents' Day, Memorial Day, _____

8. do, ti, la, sol, _____

9. Argentina, Bolivia, Brazil, Chile, Columbia, _____

10. 5, 6 ⅔, 8 ⅓, 10, 11 ⅔, _____

11. 0, 7, 6, 13, 12, 19, 18, 25, _____

12. b, e, h, k, n, q, _____

13. Point, 40, 30, 15, _____

14. Octagon, heptagon, hexagon, pentagon, quadrilateral, _____

15. Eight, five, four, nine, one, seven, _____

16. Monday, Thursday, Sunday, Wednesday, Saturday, _____

17. September, February, July, December, _____

18. Anthony, Kennedy, Washington, Roosevelt, _____

19. 54, 108, 36, 72, 24, 48, _____

20. 1, 1, 2, 3, 5, 8, 13, _____

21. Touchdown with 2-point conversion, touchdown with 1-point conversion, touchdown with no conversion, field goal, _____

22. 720, 360, 120, 30, 6, _____

23. I, II, III, IV, V, VI, VII, VIII, _____

24. Ace, eight, five, four, jack, _____

25. Kindergarten, Elementary, Middle, High, Bachelor, Master, _____

Day Six: Verbal Teasers

Skills: Left Brain
Number of Exercises: Two

In Exercise One you will be presented with a word or clusters of words that have a secondary meaning. Each word or word cluster represents a familiar phrase. The following two examples are for Exercise One only.

Example One

What familiar phrase might this word represent?

JET

Answer: Jumbo Jet

Example Two

Find the familiar phrase hidden in the word cluster.

<u>Standing</u>
MISS

Answer: Mis<u>under</u>standing

Exercise One

Find the familiar phrase hidden in each of the word clusters. Check your answers at the end of the chapter

1. often
   often
   often   not
   often
   often

2. quarter,quarter,quarter,quarter,quarter
   quarter,quarter,quarter,quarter,quarter
   quarter,quarter,quarter,quarter,quarter

3.   Pants
          Pants   Pants
   Pants   Kick   Pants
          Pants   Pants
                Pants

4. <u>SOMEWHERE</u>
   THE RAINBOW

5.   R   R
        O   O
            A
        D   D
      S   S

6. ƎꓵUTЯOꟻ

7. HEARTED

8. HEAVEN
   <u>– PENNIES</u>

Exercise Two

Use verbal and visual clues to solve the following brainteasers. Check your answers at the end of the chapter.

1. What common saying is represented by these "big" words?
The most tender passions and feelings cause the rotational force propelling this inhabited planet.

2. Which name doesn't belong and why?
Larry, Kirsty, Jane, David, Amy

3. What part of London is in France?

4. What state is round on both sides but high in the middle?

5. What's at the center of the earth?

Day Seven: Diabolical Dartboard

Skills: Left Brain

Number of Exercises: One

Exercise One

Henry had a special dartboard made with the numbers put in a certain logical order, but the craftspeople made a (reasonable) mistake by putting one of the numbers in the wrong place in the sequence. Which number is out of place, and where should it have been placed? If you get stuck, read the upside down clue below.

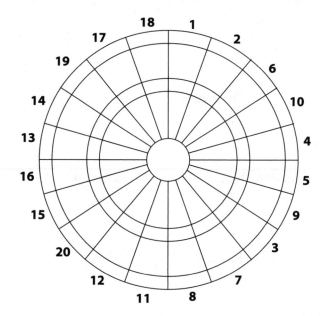

Clue: Turn the numbers into the words they represent (e.g., the number 2 is represented by the word *two*. *Turn* the numbers into words. Find the rule that orders the sequence. Then find the number that is out of place.

Dr. Brainfit's Advice Column

Dear Dr. Brainfit,

My spouse is after me to stop using antiperspirant products containing aluminum. She says if I keep using my deodorant I will end up with Alzheimer's disease. I have been using the same deodorant, which contains some aluminum, for twenty-five years with no ill effects. Is there something more I should know about aluminum?

Ben from Kansas

Dear Ben,

Your wife is wise to be cautious. Recent studies have linked aluminum toxicity to Alzheimer's disease.

Alzheimer's and Aluminum Toxicity

While the role of aluminum toxicity in promoting Alzheimer's disease is still being debated, there is a great deal of evidence to suggest a connection between Alzheimer's and aluminum toxicity. Autopsies of the brains of people with Alzheimer's have revealed increased levels of aluminum and silicon. An article in the British medical journal, *The Lancet*, "Geographical Relation Between Alzheimer's Disease and Aluminum in Drinking Water," summarizes the results of a study that shows a statistically significant correlation between aluminum in drinking water and the risk of developing Alzheimer's disease.

Aluminum is the third most common element in the earth's crust. We are continuously exposed to aluminum in everyday living. Acid rain draws aluminum out of the soil and into drinking water. Aluminum is a common additive in certain brands of baking powers and instant chocolate mixes. It is also found in drinks packaged in aluminum cans, dandruff shampoos, cosmetic

▼

products, pots and pans, certain over-the-counter pharmaceutical products, and many foils and wraps. Some scientists are particularly worried about spray antiperspirants because brain autopsy studies of Alzheimer's patients have shown a high proportion of senile plaque in the "smelling" lobes of the brain. Coincidentally, one of the first signs of Alzheimer's disease is a degraded sense of smell.

Despite the recent findings linking aluminum to Alzheimer's disease, our human body has many natural defense mechanisms and systems that protect us from toxic substances like aluminum. Most of our daily intake of aluminum is eliminated by healthy kidneys. The brain is normally protected from toxic substances by a membrane called the blood-brain barrier. Additionally, there are many commonsense things we can do to eliminate our exposure to aluminum, including:

- Substitute porcelain and glass cookware for aluminum cookware.
- Avoid ingestible forms of aluminum found in food additives.
- Avoid pharmaceutical products with high aluminum content, including many antacids, certain diarrhea products, buffered aspirin, and certain antiperspirants.
- Avoid spray forms of aluminum, which can be inhaled.
- Get information on aluminum content in water studies for your community.
- Read the labels of all products you buy and screen out harmful products.

Solutions

Day One, Exercise One:

1. rain, rein	10. mooed, mood	19. brake, break
2. toe, tow	11. two, to	20. pain, pane
3. be, bee	12. boarder, border	21. main, mane
4. no, know	13. days, daze	22. hoarse, horse
5. butt, but	14. buy, by	23. mined, mind
6. feet, feat	15. might, mite	24. moose, mousse
7. please, pleas	16 tied, tide	25. some, sum
8. great, grate	17. flees, fleas	
9. bow, bough	18. wait, weight	

Day One, Exercise Two:

1. empty
2. gentle
3. constructive
4. winter
5. troublesome
6. violent
7. thoughtful
8. neat
9. angry
10. fuse

Day Two, Exercise One:

1. envied	7. violin
2. broken	8. ablaze
3. iodine	9. crunch
4. people	10. omelet
5. eraser	11. rhythm
6. soothe	12. goalie

Day Two, Exercise Two:

1. Find the word that is not a breed of dog.
   a. spaniel
   b. shepherd
   c. beagle
   d. shark
   e. terrier

2. Find the word that is not a type of flower.
   a. marigold
   b. turtle
   c. tulip
   d. petunia
   e. violet

3. Find the word that is not a type of bird.
   a. pigeon
   b. osprey

4. Find the word that is not a name of an ocean.
   a. Atlantic
   b. Indian

c. peacock

d. peanut

e. sparrow

c. Arctic

d. river

e. Pacific

5. Find the word that is not a language.

a. accent

b. English

c. Hebrew

d. Chinese

e. Swahili

Day Three, Exercise One: sake, skate, basket, setback

Day Three, Exercise Two: Nightingale, Kingfisher

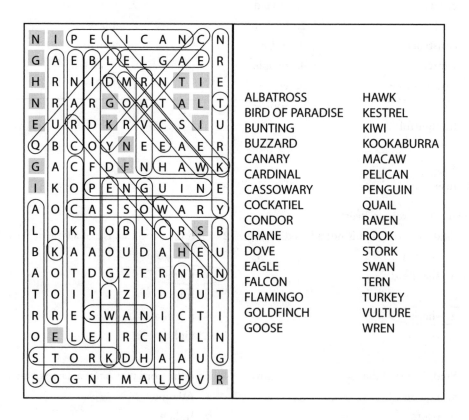

ALBATROSS
BIRD OF PARADISE
BUNTING
BUZZARD
CANARY
CARDINAL
CASSOWARY
COCKATIEL
CONDOR
CRANE
DOVE
EAGLE
FALCON
FLAMINGO
GOLDFINCH
GOOSE

HAWK
KESTREL
KIWI
KOOKABURRA
MACAW
PELICAN
PENGUIN
QUAIL
RAVEN
ROOK
STORK
SWAN
TERN
TURKEY
VULTURE
WREN

Day Four, Exercise One:

1. Each word in Column A has three of one letter.
2. Each word in Column A forms a compound word by adding *man*.
3. Column A is names of magazines.
4. Column A is names of NFL quarterbacks.
5. Column A is composed of prime numbers.
6. Words in Column A are types of insects.
7. Each word in Column A can be used to describe time.
8. Column A is a list of cartoonists.
9. Column A is names of types of pasta.
10. Songs in Column A are all from the children's televisions show *Sesame Street*.
11. Column A is comprised of words you'd hear in Australia.
12. Words in Column A, when they follow the word *doctor*, form a recognizable name.

Day Four, Exercise Two: All the words can be used to create colors: hot pink, off white, powder blue, royal blue, jet black, lime green, steel gray, flame red.

Day Five, Exercise One:

1. Johnson (U.S. presidents in reverse order)
2. 26 (increase by 3)
3. R (every other consonant)
4. 5:50 (increase by 50 minutes)
5. Vermont (American states listed in reverse alphabetical order)
6. 96 (doubling)
7. Independence Day (U.S. national holidays in calendar order)
8. Fa (musical notes in reverse order)
9. Ecuador (South American countries in alphabetical order)
10. 13 ⅓ (increase by 1 ⅔)
11. 24 (increase by 7, decrease by 1, repeat)
12. t (increase by three)
13. Love or Zero (points scored in tennis, in reverse order)
14. Triangle (names of polygons in decreasing order of the number of sides)

Day Five, Exercise One: (cont.)

15. Six (numerals in alphabetical order)
16. Tuesday (increase by three days)
17. May (increase by five months)

18. Jefferson (faces on U.S. coins in descending order of coin value)
19. 16 (double, divide by 3, repeat)
20. 21 (sum of the two previous numbers, also called a Fibonacci Series)
21. Safety (scoring in football ranked from the most points to the least)
22. 1 (divide by 1 more than the previous number)
23. IX (Roman numerals)
24. King (value of playing cards, listed in alphabetical order)
25. Doctorate (next highest degree in formal education)

Day Six, Exercise One:

1. More often than not
2. Close quarters
3. Kick in the pants
4. Somewhere over the rainbow
5. Crossroads
6. Reversal of fortune
7. Broken (or half) hearted
8. Pennies from heaven

Day Six, Exercise Two:

1. Love makes the world go round
2. Kirsty (it doesn't contain the letter *a*)
3. The letter *n*
4. Ohio
5. The letter *r*

Day Seven, Exercise One: The numbers are arranged in order by the length of their words, and then by their numeric value. The three-letter numbers are first, and are ordered one, two, six, and ten. They are followed by the four-letters numbers, and so on. The incorrectly placed number is eighteen, which the craftspeople might have misspelled as *eightteen*. Eighteen should go between fourteen and nineteen.

Chapter Ten

Mental Agility Challenges for the Right Brain

"The more you use your brain, the more brain you will have to use."
—GEORGE A. DORSEY

Brain Dominance

If you are **left brain dominant** you prefer to process information in a logical, sequential manner. The left hemisphere of the brain is the seat of language; hence people who have a left brain preference tend to be strong in verbal logic and reasoning. If you are **right brain dominant** your strengths will be in visual and spatial reasoning. People with a dominant right brain prefer to process information intuitively, holistically, and randomly. Brain dominance refers to our thinking and learning preference and is not an absolute. Similarly, just because you have a dominant eye or hand does not mean you cannot use and strengthen your non-dominant hand or eye—so it follows that we can and should work to use and strengthen the non-dominant side of our brain.

To determine the balance between your brain hemispheres and which side of your brain is dominant, take the following Hemispheric Dominance Inventory.[1]

Hemispheric Dominance Inventory

For each item, circle the letter "a" or "b," whichever most closely describes your preference. You must choose either "a" or "b," you cannot choose both. If you are not sure, consider what your response would be if the situation described were stressful, difficult, or new.

1. Are you usually running late for class or other appointments?
   a. Yes
   b. No

2. When taking a test, do you prefer that questions be . . .
   a. Objective (true/false multiple choice, matching)
   b. Subjective (discussion or essay question)

3. When making decisions . . .
   a. You go with your gut feeling.
   b. You carefully weigh each option.

4. When relating an event to a friend . . .
   a. You go straight to the main point and then fill in details.
   b. You tell many details before revealing the conclusion.

5. Do you have a place for everything and everything in its place?
   a. Yes
   b. No

6. When faced with a major change in life, you are . . .
   a. Excited
   b. Nervous

7. Your work style is like this:
   a. You concentrate on one task at a time until it is complete.
   b. You usually juggle several things at once.

8. Can you tell approximately how much time has passed without a watch?
   a. Yes
   b. No

9. Which is easier for you to understand?
   a. Algebra
   b. Geometry

10. It is easier for you to remember people's . . .
    a. Names
    b. Faces

11. When learning a new piece of equipment you . . .
    a. Jump in and wing it (the manual is a last resort).
    b. Carefully read the instruction manual before beginning.

12. When someone is speaking, you respond to . . .
    a. What is being said (words).
    b. How it is being said (tone, tempo, volume, emotion).

13. When speaking, do you use hand gestures?
    a. Few gestures (very seldom use hands when talking).
    b. Many gestures (couldn't talk with hands tied).

14. What is your desk, work area, or laundry area like?
    a. Neat and organized
    b. Cluttered with stuff I might need

15. When asked your opinion you . . .
    a. Immediately say what's on your mind (often with foot in mouth).
    b. Think before you speak.

16. Do you do your best thinking sitting at your desk or walking around or lying down?
    a. Sitting at your desk
    b. Walking around or lying down

17. When reading a magazine do you . . .
    a. Jump in wherever it looks most interesting.
    b. Start at page one and read in sequential order.

18. When you're shopping and see something you want to buy . . .
    a. You save up until you have the money.
    b. You charge it.

19. If you were hanging a picture on a wall, you would . . .
    a. Carefully measure to be sure it is centered and straight.
    b. Put it where it looks right and move it if necessary.

Left Brain Preferences:
1b, 2a, 3b, 4b, 5a, 6b, 7a, 8a, 9a, 10a, 11b, 12a, 13a, 14a, 15b, 16a, 17b, 18a, 19a

Right Brain Preferences:
1a, 2b, 3a, 4a, 5b, 6a, 7b, 8b, 9b, 10b, 11a, 12b, 13b, 14b, 15a, 16b, 17a, 18b, 19b

 ## Ideas for Right Brain Stimulation

1. Use colored pens and colored Post-it Notes as visual markers for things you want to remember.
2. Capture your ideas as quick sketches.
3. Use picture symbols for memory messages.
4. Pick a common object (for example, a paper clip) and brainstorm new and creative ways to use it.
5. Pick a room in your house and think up creative ways to give the room a face-lift.

6. Start collecting something that interests you (such as sea shells, buttons, pill boxes, or rocks) and find a creative way to display them in your home.

7. Work with brain games that involve patterns like Rubik's Cube, mazes, jigsaw puzzles, and dominoes.

8. Create collages using different materials each time (e.g., different fabrics, bird seeds, colored tissue paper).

9. Take up a visual-pattern-oriented hobby like sewing, embroidery, painting, or photography.

10. Take up a hobby that involves making things with your hands, like woodworking, pottery, model airplanes, or sculpting.

11 Take an art history class.

12. Play visually oriented video games.

13. Take a class in acting improvisation.

14. Write a simple story for children, then illustrate it, to create a picture book.

What's the Workout Rationale?

Knowing whether you are left brain or right brain dominant can help you in many aspects of your life, such as:

- Customizing your work and learning environment to suit your preferred learning and thinking modes.
- Choosing a career that aligns with the natural strengths of your preferred thinking mode and skills.
- Selecting brain fitness activities that preserve your dominant brain strengths and strengthen your nondominant brain abilites.

In Chapter Nine, you engaged in exercises designed to stimulate and strengthen the left side of your brain. Now it's time to cross over to the right side of your brain for a complete mental agility workout.

Let's Work Out!

Ready to begin? This week's exercises all have a strong visual-spatial orientation. If this is not your dominant brain preference, don't worry, as there are lots of examples and clues.

Weekly Exercise Planner

Here is your weekly planner for this week's right brain workout.

Day	Exercise Name	Skill	Pages
Day One	Sequences	Right Brain	239–240
Day Two	Reconstruction	Right Brain	241–242
Day Three	Rotations	Right Brain	243–244
Day Four	Compare & Contrast	Right Brain	245–246
Day Five	Optical Illusions	Right Brain	247–248
Day Six	Connections	Right Brain	249
Day Seven	Maze Craze	Right Brain	250–252

*Note: Solutions for this week's mental agility exercises are located at the end of this chapter.

Day One: Sequences

Skills: Right Brain

Number of Exercises: Two

Some things in life follow a sequence. In the following two exercises, the key to the sequence is in the visual pattern. Find the rule that orders the pattern of the sequence. Then circle the figure that completes the sequence. Choose from figures a–d.

Exercise One

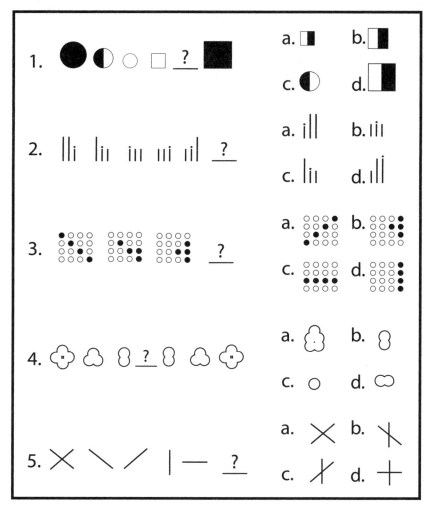

Exercise Two

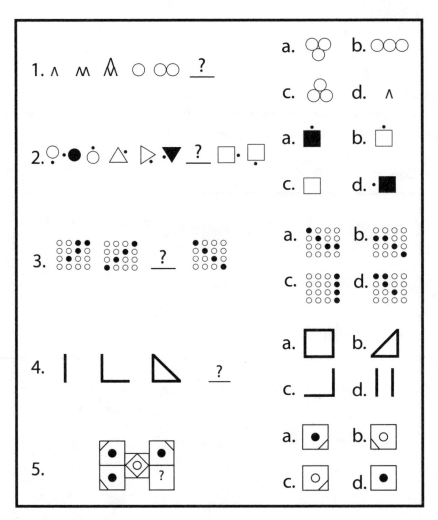

Day Two: Reconstruction

Skills: Right Brain

Number of Exercises: Two

Exercise One

Which sets of pieces can be used to reconstruct figures 1 and 2 on the left? Circle the correct set of pieces on the right.

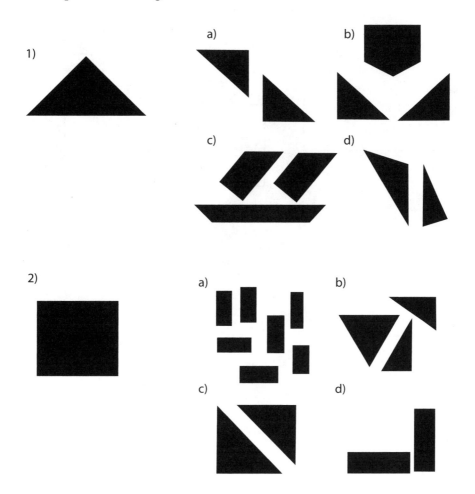

Clue: If you get stuck, make an enlarged photocopy of the pieces, cut them out, and manually manipulate them to reconstruct the figures.

Exercise Two

Fit the six pieces into the box so that none of the pieces overlap, no piece covers the black square already in the box, and so that all the white dots are adjacent to a black dot on another piece or the black square. You may find it helpful to make an enlarged photocopy of this exercise and cut out the pieces so that you can manually rotate them.

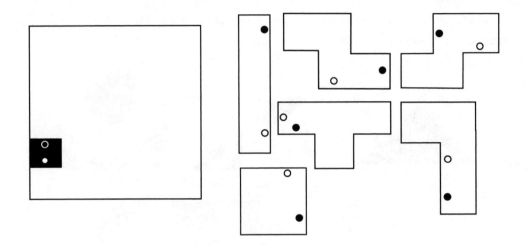

Day Three: Rotations

Skills: Right Brain

Number of Exercises: Two

Exercise One

Circle the house plan on the right that is a rotation of the original house plan on the left.

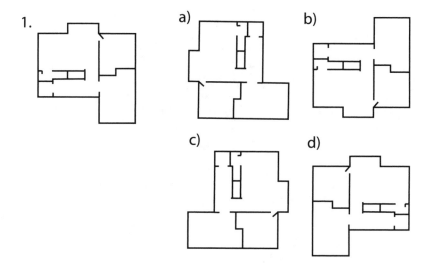

Exercise Two

Circle the figure in each sequence that does not belong. If you solve one, you've broken the code and you can solve them all.

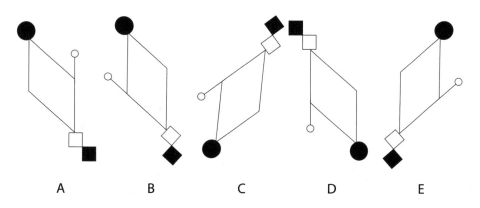

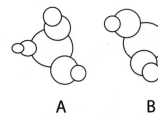
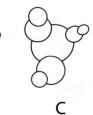
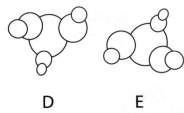

A   B   C   D   E

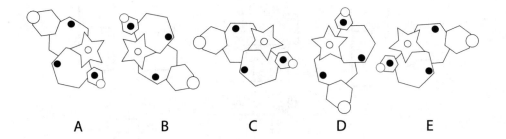

A   B   C   D   E

Day Four: Compare & Contrast

Skills: Right Brain
Number of Exercises: Two

Exercise One

An artist was commissioned to draw two identical flower vases for twin sisters. But, he made some mistakes. The twins have refused to pay him until he corrects these mistakes. See if you can help the artist pick out the ten features that make the two drawings dissimilar. Circle the dissimilar features in the drawing on the right. Check your answers at the end of the chapter.

Exercise Two

Study the farm scene for things that seem odd. There are five oddities hidden in the branches of the trees and five interspersed in the rest of the picture. Circle the ten odd elements in the farm scene. Check your answers at the end of the chapter.

Day Five: Optical Illusions

Skills: Right Brain
Number of Exercises: Two

Not everything is as it first seems. How we comprehend the world around us depends on the brain "filters" we use. In the following two exercises, you will use different brain filters to discover some interesting optical illusions.

Exercise One

The picture below is a copy of a well-known painting. The painting is an optical illusion because there are two images in the painting. One image is of a young woman and the other image is of an old woman. See if you can find the two images. Turning the picture upside down may help. If you are stumped, use the clues below to help you unravel the optical illusion.

Clues: Hear are some clues to help you find the two images. The young woman's ear is the old woman's eye. The young woman's chin is the old woman's nose. The young woman's nose is the old woman's wart. The young woman's necklace is the old woman's mouth.

Exercise Two

The following drawing has a hidden word. See if you can find the word hidden in the face.

Day Six: Connections

Skills: Right Brain
Number of Exercises: Two

Exercise One

The following Nine Dot Problem is an old classic that requires you to use spatial-relationship skills. The task is to draw a line through all nine of the dots with four straight lines without taking your pencil off the page. No line should double back over another line. Each dot must be on at least one line. To solve the problem you will need to think "outside of the box."

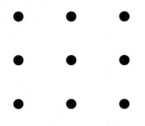

Exercise Two

This Squares Count Problem is another classic right brain problem. How many squares are in the following figure? Be sure to look for all the squares within the square.

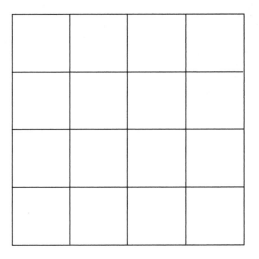

Day Seven: Maze Craze

Skills: Right Brain

Number of Exercises: Three

Have fun with following three mazes. Your goal is to find your way through the labyrinth beginning at the starting point and ending at the finish point. The mazes progress from the least to the most difficult. You can work on all three, or pick one for today's workout.

Exercise One

Start

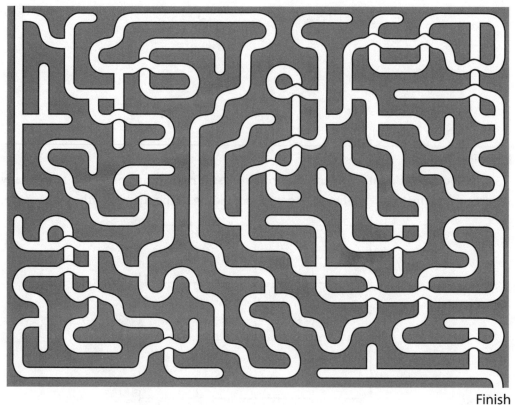

Finish

Exercise Two

Start

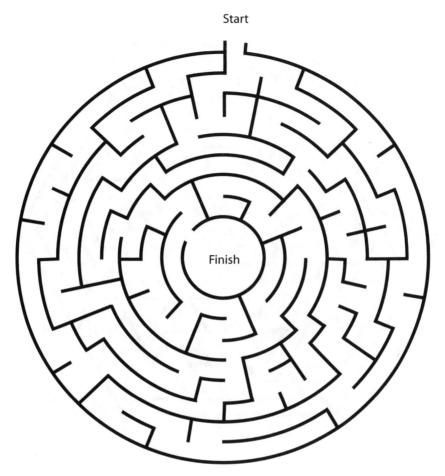

Finish

Exercise Three

Dr. Brainfit's Advice Column

Dear Dr. Brainfit,

Americans have become a nation of coffee drinkers. It seems like there is a Dunkin' Donuts or Starbucks on every corner. Has anyone studied the effect of caffeine on the mind and the body?

Liz from Toronto

Dear Liz,

Coffee is definitely the drink "du jour" and the trend shows no signs of slowing down. Fortunately, there are research projects studying the effects of caffeine on the mind and the body.

Caffeine—Fuel Up or Not?

A research team led by Dr. Lee Ryan at the University of Arizona conducted a study to determine the effects of caffeine on memory in adults aged sixty-five and older who considered themselves "morning people."[2] The researchers found that older adults who drank a twelve-ounce cup of regular coffee before taking a memory test in the morning and in the afternoon performed better than their peers who drank a cup of decaffeinated coffee before each testing period. Additionally, the caffeine drinkers showed no noticeable decline in memory throughout the day. In an interview, Dr. Ryan explained that caffeine stimulates many regions of the brain. Areas of the brain that regulate wakefulness, arousal, mood, and concentration are especially sensitive to even low doses of caffeine. She went on to say, "We suspect that this accounts for the increase in performance. If so, caffeine would have an impact on a wide variety of cognitive functions, not just memory."[3]

In a study of a completely different nature, Dr. Allan Conney, a professor of cancer and leukemia research at Rutgers University, found that a skin lotion spiked with caffeine, or with another compound found in green tea, can reduce by more than half the number of cancer tumors on the skin of hairless mice exposed to severe levels of ultraviolet radiation.[4]

So is it all good news when it comes to caffeine consumption? First, it is important to note that the research findings with regard to memory improvement may not apply to younger adults unless they are particularly tired or sleep-deprived. Also the studies looked at people who were already coffee drinkers with no ill effects from caffeine. It did not look at populations who have experienced negative effects of caffeine, such as withdrawal headaches, shakiness, anxiety, or decreased concentration. Additionally, Dr. Jim Lane, a researcher at Duke University Medical School, warns that caffeine always raises blood pressure and that the excessive amounts of coffee many Americans consume each day can raise blood pressure enough to increase the risk of heart attack or stroke. As with so many things, the nutritional wisdom seems to be to enjoy your daily coffee, but in moderation, and consider saving your caffeine consumption for those times during the day when you need a mental boost.

Solutions

Day One, Exercise One:
1. b
2. a
3. d
4. c
5. d

Day One, Exercise Two:
1. c
2. b
3. d
4. a
5. a

Day Two, Exercise One:
1. d
2. b

Day Two, Exercise Two:

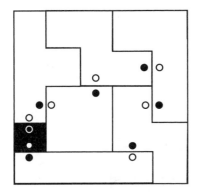

Day Three, Exercise One: c

Day Three, Exercise Two: b, c, e. The figure that does not belong is an inversion of figure A. All the other figures are rotations of figure A. If you get stuck, photocopy the figures, cut them out, and manually rotate them.

Day Four, Exercise One: There are nine dissimilarities between the pictures. The flower vase on the right has the following differences:
1. more black coloring on the vase
2. extra "dash line" to the bottom left of the vase
3. extra flower hanging down at the bottom left of the arrangement
4. extra black leaf juts out of the left side of the arrangement
5. extra flower sticks up from the top of the arrangement
6. center black flower is missing white petal overlay
7. top center flower has an extra leaf on the left side of the stalk

255

8. top white flower has one less petal
9. bottom right flower has an extra leaf on the stalk

Day Four, Exercise Two: The farm scene has ten oddities. The five farm tools hidden in the trees are: a saw, a garden hose, a hat, scissors, and spade. The five additional oddities in the scene are: the letter "N" hidden in the fence, the numbers 1, 2, and 3 in the field, the rake hidden in the field, the eye on the car headlight, and the flower basket, which holds apples instead of flowers.

Day Five, Exercise Two: The hidden word is "Liar."

Day Six, Exercise One:

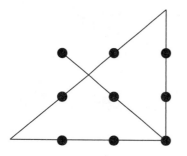

Day Six, Exercise Two: Using all possible combinations of squares, there are thirty squares.

Day Seven, Exercise One:

Day Seven, Exercise Two:

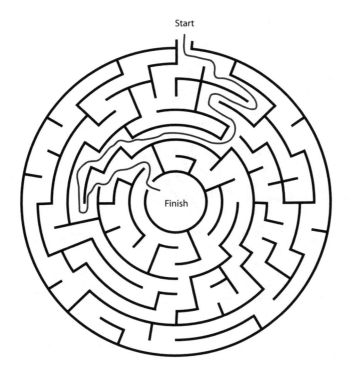

Day Seven, Exercise Three:

Chapter Eleven

Maintain Your Brain

"The best way to predict the future is to create it."
—PETER F. DRUCKER

On the Other Side of Young

Have you ever had a defining moment when it suddenly hit you that you are no longer young? It happens when you least expect it and usually has nothing to do with chronological age markers like birthdays. Perhaps you are reading the paper and wonder why they started shrinking the print. Maybe you look in the mirror and notice those first gray hairs. Perhaps you stop midconversation, unable to recall the name of the movie you saw last week. Some other little reminders of getting older are listed below. Do any of these apply to you?[1]

1. Does the idea of lying on the floor to watch TV strike you as uncomfortable?
2. Do you groan a little when you bend over to get up?
3. Have your children studied events in history that you lived through?
4. Does your little black book contain mostly names ending in M.D.?

5. Do you have too much room in the house and not enough room in the medicine cabinet?
6. Are you using tweezers on your chin instead of your eyebrows?
7. Do you burn the midnight oil until 9:30 P.M.?
8. Does it take twice as long to look half as good?
9. Do you turn out the lights for economic reasons rather than romantic ones?
10. Do you look forward to a dull evening?
11. Do you sing along to elevator music?
12. Do you shop for comfortable shoes rather than cool ones?

If you answered yes to two or more questions, I hate to burst your bubble but you are on the other side of young.

Successful Aging

Many of us who are on the other side of young are asking questions about how to achieve a good quality of life as we age. Is it possible to age with grace and vigor? What influence or control do we have over successful aging? As the eighty million baby boomers begin to gray, the population of individuals considered to be senior citizens is exploding. Statisticians predict that life expectancy by the middle of the twenty-first century could be well into the nineties, with as many as 600,000 individuals in the United States living past one hundred. To prepare for this explosion, scientists and gerontologists are working hard to uncover the controllable factors that will promote successful aging. Longitudinal studies of aging populations and cutting edge neuroscience research are dispelling old myths about aging and redefining what it means to age successfully. What we are learning about successful aging is encouraging. Despite our genetic proclivities, there are many things we can do to significantly influence how we age. Each study or research project has added to our inventory of knowledge regarding the promise of positive aging.

How Mental Functions Change with Age

Topping our list of questions about aging are concerns about mental decline. Losing the ability to think quickly, reason clearly, and remember accurately is one of our biggest age-related fears. So what have scientists learned about changes in cognitive function as we age?

While some mental functions do decline with age, there are many positive factors that offset these changes. Older adults do experience a reduction in processing speed, the amount of time it takes to learn new information. It takes longer to learn a new language at sixty than at twenty. Fortunately, most of the things we do on a daily basis do not depend on how quickly we process information. It's interesting to note however, that older adults who go back to school often get better grades than when they were younger. Many seniors say this is because they do not have the social and financial pressures they had when they were younger and so can devote their full attention to learning. Another mental function affected by the aging process is concentration. Seniors find it harder to concentrate when they are multitasking or when they are faced with interruptions and distractions.

Researchers have found that despite these minor cognitive declines, there are many areas in which older adults outperform the young. In several research tests, older adults outperformed young adults in reading comprehension when the material to be read was relevant to their lives. They also did just as well as young adults in reasoning tests when the problems to be solved had real-world significance and an emotional element. And researchers have documented gains in vocabulary and wisdom well into our seventies.

With regard to changes in memory, the biggest change is that on occasion it takes a little longer to recall certain information. Some seniors refer to this as the "tip of the tongue" phenomenon. We know the information, but we just can't call it up on demand. Other types of memory show little or no decline as we age. When presented with information they have heard or seen, seniors recall and recognize the information about as well as younger people. Older adults also maintain a good working memory for performing the tasks of everyday living. And of course, we know that actively exercising the brain will preserve and strengthen our cognitive functions.

Assessing Your Gains

You have been actively exercising your mind and your memory for several weeks now through your participation in the *Brainfit* program. Significant changes in memory and mental agility occur over time and can be measured. Just as with physical exercise, the longer you engage in a regular and ongoing brain exercise program, the greater the gains.

In Chapter One you took three pre-assessments, two for memory and one for mental agility. Let's measure some of the gains you've achieved as a result of your nine week investment in the *Brainfit* program by retaking these assessments.

Subjective Memory Post-Assessment

In Chapter One you took the Subjective Memory Self-Assessment. Now, you'll retake this assessment to learn how your memory competence and confidence have improved. Do not look back at your old scores until you have completed the new assessment. The assessment procedure and questions are the same. You will circle a number between 1 and 7 that best reflects your overall judgment about your memory. Ready to begin?

How Often Do These Present a Problem For You?

Remembering Who	No Problem					Severe Problem	
Names of people	1	2	3	4	5	6	7
Names of places (e.g., restaurants, stores)	1	2	3	4	5	6	7
Titles (e.g., books, movies)	1	2	3	4	5	6	7

Remembering What							
To complete errands	1	2	3	4	5	6	7
To perform household chores	1	2	3	4	5	6	7
To buy something at the supermarket	1	2	3	4	5	6	7
To finish a task I started	1	2	3	4	5	6	7

Remembering How Many							
Phone numbers I use often	1	2	3	4	5	6	7
Important personal numbers (e.g., license, security codes)	1	2	3	4	5	6	7
How to balance my checkbook	1	2	3	4	5	6	7

Remembering When							
Appointments and meetings	1	2	3	4	5	6	7
Special occasions (e.g., birthdays)	1	2	3	4	5	6	7
To take medications on time	1	2	3	4	5	6	7

Remembering Where		No Problem				Severe Problem	
Where I put things (e.g., keys, TV remote)	1	2	3	4	5	6	7
Where I parked my car	1	2	3	4	5	6	7
Directions to familiar places	1	2	3	4	5	6	7

Remembering in Conversations							
What I was just saying	1	2	3	4	5	6	7
Whether I told someone something	1	2	3	4	5	6	7
Whether someone told me something	1	2	3	4	5	6	7
Finding the right word	1	2	3	4	5	6	7

Scoring Process

To assess your gains, complete Steps One and Two below. In Step One, you will determine your average score for this assessment and compare it to your average score on the baseline assessment in Chapter One on pages 10 – 12. In Step Two, you will compare your individual scores on each of the items on this assessment to your individual scores on the baseline assessment items in Chapter One.

Step One

1. Add up the total score of all the items you circled.
2. Divide your total score by 20 (the total number of items)
3. Determine your average score
4. Compare your average score to your average score on the baseline assessment

Score	Interpretation
1	You have no perceived memory problems
2–3	You perceive mild memory problems
4–5	You perceive moderate memory problems
6–7	You perceive major memory problems

Step Two

1. Compare your individual item scores on this assessment with your individual item scores on the baseline assessment.
2. Circle all individual items for which your score improved (lower number).
3. Total the number items for which your score improved.

Interpreting Your Gains

To assess your personal gains, ask yourself the following questions:

1. Do you see improvement in your overall average score?
2. Do you see improvement in the individual item scores? How many individual items show improvement?
3. Do you see improvement in the scores for a particular category? Which categories?
4. Do you feel more confident about your memory and your ability to improve your memory?

Answering yes to any of these questions means you have personally gained as a result of your participation in the *Brainfit* program. Be proud of your accomplishments and celebrate your successes. Answering yes to two or more questions means you perceive significant gains. The best part is that these gains are just a beginning. Just as continuing to work out at the gym increases your gains, so does continuing to work out your brain. You are on the path to a healthier and stronger brain. Keep up the good work!

Objective Memory Post-Assessment

Now let's take a look at your gains on the Objective Memory Assessment. Everything will be same, except for one thing. This time, before you begin, you will *determine your memory strategy*. Which of the fundamental memory skills do you want to use to better remember the words? For example, you might link the words, in a row or a column, together in a picture or story. Once you've decided which memory skills you'll use, you are ready to retake the Objective Memory Assessment that follows.

Read through the list of words just once, and only once, concentrating on each word. Then cover the list and write down as many words as you can remember on a sheet of paper.

Box	Shout	King
Knock	Knee	Dance
Lose	Present	Licorice
Shoe	Banana	Dog

Interpreting Your Gains

How did you do? Compare the number of words you remembered in this assessment with the number of words you remembered in the Chapter One baseline assessment.

How many more words did you remember? If you remembered the same number of words did your memory time improve? Which memory techniques did you use?

Mental Agility Post-Assessment

In Chapter One, you took a mental agility pre-assessment similar to the one that follows. Now you'll retake the assessment to see if your confidence and competence have improved. The items in each row below form a series. Each series is based on a predictable pattern or rule. Find the rule or pattern, then fill in the answer that completes the series. For the graphic illustrations, select the letter which corresponds to the shape which completes the series.

When you are ready to begin, **set the timer for five minutes.** Stop when the timer goes off. Read the answer key at the end of the chapter and circle the items you answered correctly.

1. 0, 1, 3, 6, 10, 15, 21, _____

2. Kennedy, Johnson, Nixon, Nixon, Carter, Reagan, _____

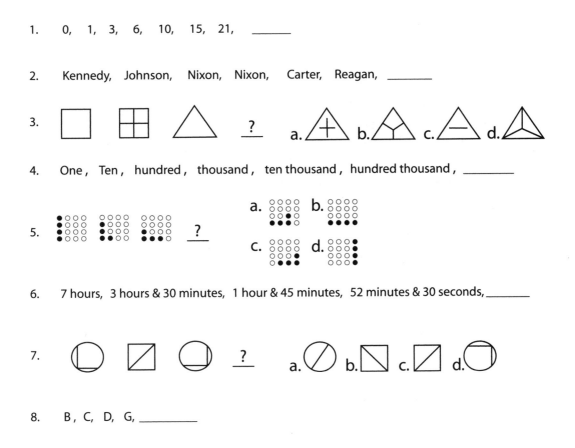

3.

4. One, Ten, hundred, thousand, ten thousand, hundred thousand, _____

5.

6. 7 hours, 3 hours & 30 minutes, 1 hour & 45 minutes, 52 minutes & 30 seconds, _____

7.

8. B, C, D, G, _____

9.

10. Say, you, by, dawn's, light, _____

Interpreting Your Score

Compare the number of items you answered correctly in the Mental Agility Post assessment to the number of items you answered correctly on the Mental Agility Pre-Assessment in Chapter One. Did you answer more items correctly in the allotted time frame? Did the problem solving get easier? Were you able to complete each series more quickly? Was it more fun this time?

Assess Your Lifestyle

Regular brain exercise can help you to preserve, protect, and build both memory and mental agility. But brain exercise alone does not tell the whole story when it comes to brain health and successful aging. Researchers have uncovered nine key lifestyle factors that complement brain exercise and promote successful aging. These factors are summarized in the *Brainfit* Lifestyle Assessment that follows. Taking this assessment will help you pinpoint your lifestyle strengths and areas of risk. Later in this chapter you will use the results of this assessment to help you build a blueprint for a healthier body and brain by completing the *Brainfit* Action Plan.

Brainfit Lifestyle Assessment

Place a check mark next to each factor you are currently managing well. Place an "X" next to those factors you are not currently managing well.

1. Manage your Numbers_____

What's good for your heart is good for your brain. High blood pressure, heart disease, and stroke are risk factors for dementia. Work with your doctor to control body weight, blood pressure, cholesterol levels, and blood sugar levels. If you are taking multiple medications, consult with your doctor about the combined effect of these medications on your memory, mood, and mental acuity.

2. Feed your Brain_____

Good nutrition is critical to brain health. A low-fat, low-cholesterol diet will help protect your heart and your brain. A diet rich in dark green vegetables and fruits, which contain antioxidants, helps fight off free radicals and protects brain cells. Omega-3 fatty acids found in fish contain properties that boost both mood and memory. Supplement your diet with the antioxidant vitamins E and C, as well as vitamin B12 (folic acid).

3. Manage Environmental Toxins_____

Scientists have long suspected that environmental toxins play a role in neuro-degenerative disorders, such as Alzheimer's disease, Parkinson's disease, and multiple sclerosis. Two known neurotoxins that have received a lot of negative press lately are mercury and aluminum. The FDA issued a warning recently advising pregnant women to avoid eating fish high in mercury content in order to protect their unborn children. Types of fish that have been cited as high in mercury content include shark, swordfish, king mackerel, tilefish, bluefish, and tuna. Other common sources of mercury to avoid include old-fashioned thermometers and some amalgams used in dental fillings.

Aluminum, another environmental toxin, is strongly suspected of playing a role in brain cell degeneration, and it has been linked to Alzheimer's disease. Common environmental sources of aluminum include unfiltered drinking water, food additives, antacids, diarrhea medications, dandruff shampoos, and underarm antiperspirants. Two simple solutions for minimizing exposure to aluminum toxins are to drink filtered water and to read the labels on foods and personal consumer products to screen out harmful products.

4. Stay Physically Active_____

Physical exercise has been proven to increase blood flow to the brain, which brings with it oxygen and nutrients essential to healthy brain function. Physical exercise also increases the circulation of endorphins, a hormone proven to boost both mood and memory. Being a couch potato is bad for your health. Get in the habit of standing more than sitting. A recent segment on the *NBC Nightly News* featured a research study in which people who are inclined to stand and fidget, rather than sit, burn significantly more calories, and are thinner than people who are inclined to sit.

A well-balanced physical fitness program has three elements: stretching, muscle toning, and cardiovascular (aerobic) exercise. If possible, start with a personal trainer who will design a customized physical fitness program appropriate for your age and current physical condition. Remember that walking is still one of the best and safest aerobic exercises. In a study reported in the March 2, 2004, issue of *Proceedings of the National Academy of Sciences*, researchers using high-tech neuroimaging observed the effects of walking on the human brain. They found that individuals who engaged in regular, brisk walks showed measurable gains in attention and decision-making skills.[2]

5. Manage Your Stress_____

Stress is part of being human. It can be triggered by both positive and negative life events, such as a wedding or a death in the family. The stress mechanism is thought to be a carryover from our primitive past, in which the body's "fight or flight" alert may have been the difference between eating bear for dinner and being eaten by a bear. In most societies today, this stress mechanism is no longer useful and, in fact, has been found to be harmful to healthy brain function. Living in a chronic state of stress produces prolonged exposure to the stress hormone, corticosterone. In studies at Stanford University headed by Dr. Robert Sapolsky, exposure to stress hormones resulted in visible shrinkage of the hippocampus, the area of the brain associated with memory and learning.[3] Some proven stress-reduction techniques include:

Having more fun
Laughing more
Engaging in regular physical exercise
Taking yoga classes
Listening to relaxation music tapes or CDs
Creating balance between work and leisure activities
Talking to others about your feelings
Getting more sleep
Drinking less caffeine
Praying and engaging in other spiritual activities

6. Live with Purpose_____

There is a strong correlation suggested, in both the MacArthur Study and the Nun Study, between successful aging and mental vigor and a life lived with purpose. Living with purpose is about being actively involved in meaningful work. It doesn't matter whether the work is paid or unpaid. What matters is that the work you engage in makes you feel productive and needed. One of the most moving tributes to living with purpose is recounted by Dr. David Snowdon in his book *Aging with Grace*. It is the description of an elderly nun whose osteoporosis is so severe she is forced to sit bent over with her head barely above her knees. Yet when Dr. Snowdon comes upon her, she is stuffing cotton balls into a cloth giraffe for the holiday crafts sale, and joking with the other nuns.

7. Live with Passion_____

Dr. Gene Cohen, author of *The Creative Age*, tells us that our older years may be our best years. He refers to a "liberation stage" that many people in their sixties and seventies experience.[4] Free of the financial and emotional burdens of raising a family, seniors can now pursue their own passions. They use this newly found sense of inner freedom to paint, write, or create new social programs. Some examples of famous people who pursued their passions in the second half of their lives include:

- Albert Einstein, who, after winning the Nobel Prize in physics at age forty-two, became a political activist, crusading against atomic weapons until his death at seventy-six.
- Grandma Moses, who first picked up a paintbrush at the age of seventy-eight, when arthritis forced her to give up her embroidery.
- Nelson Mandela, who become president of South Africa at seventy-six.
- Giuseppe Verdi, the Italian composer who produced his greatest work, *Otello*, at age seventy-four, and his final opera, *Falstaff*, at the age of eighty.

8. Stay Socially Connected_____

In both the the MacArthur Study and the Nun Study, staying socially connected appears to be an important factor in living a longer and healthier life. It has been recognized for quite some time that isolation is a powerful risk factor for poor health, depression, and suicide. As John W. Rowe and Robert L. Kahn point out in their book, *Successful Aging*, "Human beings are not meant to live alone. Talking, touching, and relating to others is essential to our well-being." In *Aging with Grace*, Dr. Snowdon cites "marriage, membership in clubs and social organizations, attending church frequently, and regular contact with friends and family" as positive life engagement factors.

9. Live a Life of Learning_____

Learning is the number one brain builder. Inflexible routine is the number one brain drainer. Studies show that older adults with higher levels of formal education have built more cognitive reserve than older adults with lower levels of formal education. Regardless of educational level, however, it is never too late to break out of the routine and create new learning opportunities. For a healthy brain, make new learning a lifelong pursuit.

Thirty Ways to Play with Your Brain

Learning can occur in formal classroom settings and lecture halls, as well as in the experiences of everyday living. Listed below are thirty ways to make new learning and new experiences part of everyday living.

1. Each week, learn the name of a different teller at your bank. Continue until you know each of the tellers' names by heart.
2. Whenever you go out to dinner, try to memorize the specials on the menu. The next day tell a friend about the specials.
3. Select a new person, place, or thing to observe in great detail every day. Study your chosen subject closely. Later in the day recall the subject by drawing it with as many details as you can remember.
4. Try to remember the titles of all the current movies that have been praised by film critics. Share your knowledge with others.
5. Try to get through your daily errands or grocery shopping without a list.
6. Read an article in a magazine or newspaper every day. When you are finished reading the article, write down the three to five main points of the story.
7. Listen to the news on your car radio or television in the morning and in the evening. Relate the news story that interested you the most to a friend.

8. Select a new genre for your next pleasure book. If you always read fiction, consider reading a nonfiction book next time.

9. Select a sentence in a magazine or newspaper. Try to make a new sentence using the words in the original sentence.

10. Take a friend to the movies. The next day tell another friend about the movie. Recount the names of the stars and the general plot.

11. Learn a new vocabulary word every day. Find ways to use the word in conversation during the day.

12. Play "Concentration" with a deck of cards. Turn the cards face down on a table. Select two cards at a time. If you make a match, pull the pair out of the deck. If not, put the cards back face down in their original position. Continue until there are no matches left to make. Time how long it takes you. Next week, see if you can beat your time.

13. Buy a jigsaw puzzle. Put the pieces together as quickly as possible. Write down how long it takes you. Next week, try it again. See if you can beat your previous time.

14. Create mini-experiments that heighten your perceptual skills. For example, have a friend lay out several objects of different sizes, shapes, and textures on the floor. Keeping your eyes shut, try to identify the objects by touch alone.

15. When eating in a gourmet restaurant, order a dish you have never tried before. See if you can guess the ingredients or spices in the dish. Then ask the waiter or waitress if you are correct.

16. When someone is having a conversation with you, rather than waiting for your turn to speak, actively listen to what the person is saying. See if you can summarize the main points back to the speaker.

17. Keep a "grateful journal." Every day, write down all the positive things that have happened that day. Say "thank you" to the people who made these things possible.

18. Listen to a new genre of music. If you normally listen to classical music, try listening to country-and-western for a day. Then use the Internet to learn three interesting facts about this new type of music.

19. See how long it takes you to memorize the words to a popular song on the radio. Next week, pick a different song to memorize; see if you can beat your original time.

20. Open up your senses to the world around you. When you go for a walk, listen to all the sounds around you. When you get home, write down all the different sounds you heard.

21. Really watch the sun set. Notice how the sky shifts and the colors change.

22. Buy some children's clay. Sculpt a vase or make an animal.

23. Brush your teeth with your nondominant hand.
24. Take a different route home from work. Go off on an adventure with no destination in mind.
25. Take something apart and put it back together.
26. Create a new floor plan. Rearrange the furniture in one of your rooms.
27. Play mental agility games on the Internet, such as Concentration, at www.brainfit.com.
28. Make up a new recipe from scratch.
29. Go to Toys "R" Us. Be a kid again. Wander the aisles and look at all the new games and gadgets. Buy yourself a new brain toy.
30. Before you go to bed, replay your day in your mind. See if you can remember the key events of your day in reverse order.

Brainfit Lifestyle Action Plan

By this time you should have lots of ideas and good intentions for making brain fitness part of your antiaging strategy. Turning these intentions into action requires a plan. The *Brainfit* Lifestyle Action Plan can help you turn your good intentions into achievable goals. The key elements of an action plan include: a) intentions or goals, b) actions to achieve goals, c) obstacles or help needed, d) time frame, and e) results achieved. Follow the steps in the Action Planning Process to complete the Action Planning Worksheet on page 275.

Action Planning Process

To create your personal *Brainfit* Lifestyle Action Plan, follow the steps below as you fill out the Action Planning Worksheet on page 275.

1. Select Your Goals

In Column A, select two or three of the Lifestyle Assessment factors on pages 266 – 270 as the focus of your goals. Select factors that you would like to manage better. Convert the factors into specific goals. Suppose, for instance, you choose the factor *Stay Physically Active*. Your specific goal might be *Start a Daily Walking Program*.

2. Identify Action Steps

In Column B, you will write down your action steps. These are the things you will do to achieve your goal. One way to think about action steps is to break them down into the following three categories:

Start Doing	I will start a walking program with my neighbors. We will walk three times a week at a brisk pace for 20 minutes a day.
Stop Doing	I will reduce the amount of time I spend sitting and watching TV.
Keep Doing	I will continue to do sit-ups.

3. Identify Obstacles and/or Help Needed

In the real world there are many things that interfere with our good intentions. Sometimes these obstacles are physical in nature. For instance, you may need transportation to get to an educational event. Other times they are emotional in nature. For instance, you may need someone who will encourage you to stay on track. We call these supportive people "action plan buddies." In Column C, write down the obstacles you will face and/or the help you will need.

4. Identify Your Time Frame for Assessing Progress

Having a time frame for working toward your goals creates a sense of urgency and commitment. In the time frame box, you will choose a time frame for assessing your progress toward your goals. At what time intervals will you check in with yourself, your doctor, and/or your action plan buddy to assess your progress? If you are working on a walking program, you may want to check progress weekly. If you are working on managing your cholesterol level, you may want to get retested every few months. In Column D, write your "check-in" time frames.

5. Capture Result

There are different ways to capture results. Results can be written as quantitative numbers (e.g., "I lost 7 lbs. in the last four months"). Results can be captured as an increase or decrease in certain types of activities or actions. (e.g., "I've stopped eating fish high in mercury," or "I'm learning how to use a computer"). Results can also be stated in terms of improved feelings (e.g., "My friends tell me I have more energy lately"). In Column E, capture the positive results you are achieving.

6. Celebrate Progress

Recognition and rewards are an important part of motivation. Be sure to celebrate your successes. When you achieve a lifestyle goal, do something really nice for yourself. You deserve it!

7. Recalibrate Your Goals

Continue to create new stretch goals for yourself. Raise the bar on a current goal or select a new goal from the Lifestyle Assessment Factors.

Action Planning Worksheet

Goals	Action/Steps	Obstacles/Help	Time Frame	Results

Staying on the *Brainfit* Circuit

There are many things you have accomplished over the last several weeks, which will help you stay on the *Brainfit* Circuit. Your accomplishments include:

1. Completing the *Brainfit* exercise workout program
2. Sharpening your memory and mental agility through weekly workouts
3. Measuring your personal memory gains
4. Taking the *Brainfit* Lifestyle Assessment
5. Creating a personal *Brainfit* Lifestyle Action Plan
6. Learning about important health issues in Dr. Brainfit's Advice Columns

As George Burns once said, "Just because we grow older doesn't mean we have to grow old." Unlike any other generation before us, we have been given a blueprint for brain fitness and successful aging. The choice is ours. Choose to be a brain gladiator.

See you at the centurion club!

Solutions:

Mental Agility

1. 28 (add 1 more than the previous increase)

2. Reagan (winners of U.S. presidential elections)

3. Shape B

4. Million (number places; also called powers of 10)

5. Shape B

6. 26 minutes and 15 seconds (half the previous amount of time)

7. Shape B

8. J (next alphabet letters drawn with curved lines)

9. Shape A

10. So (every other word in the lyrics of "The Star-Spangled Banner")

Appendix

Learning, Memory, and Neural Plasticity

Francis M. Crinella, Ph.D.

Cerebral gymnastics are not capable of improving the organization of the brain by increasing the number of cells, because it is known that the nerve cells after the embryonic period have lost the property of proliferation; but it can be admitted as very probable that mental exercise leads to a greater development of the dendritic apparatus and of the system of axonal collaterals in the most utilized cerebral regions.

—SANTIAGO RAMON Y CAJAL (1904)

Plasticity is operative when we fail to remember information that was once known— forgetting. Both memory and forgetting imply the presence of a plastic brain. Adapting to the challenges of everyday life requires learning, and learning requires memory, in one form or another.

While no more than a handful of cognitive theorists and neuroscientists have developed formal theories of memory, almost everyone has a set of beliefs about memory processes, most of them informal and unspoken intuitions about the way we learn, remember, and forget. We evaluate our own memory capacities in relation to our observations of others, from whom we develop suppositions about how our own memory systems ought to work, for example, by contrasting our memories of bygone school days with those of a classmate or by pitting our recall of the cards played in a gin rummy game against that of our opponent. We believe that certain actions are effective in augmenting our memory, for example, that the resultant grade on a history examination might have been higher had we studied for one more hour or that we might have remembered a now-forgotten phone number if we had repeated it twice aloud before attempting to store it in our brain's memory bank. But are these beliefs valid? Are intuitive notions and folk wisdom supported by fact? Do we overestimate or underestimate human memory potential?

The construct of neural plasticity is the ultimate wonder of nature—billions of molecules going through split-second changes that represent transmission of information and, remarkably, recording of the information that has been processed. Indeed, it widely believed that the brain of the typical human adult has more bits of information stored in memory than it has nerve cells, which number about 100 billion! Each bit of memory, no matter how small, is an indication that our brain has changed—plasticity.

Imbedded in the labyrinthine assembly of incoming, buffered, stored, retrieved, and outgoing neural messages is a process that we come to experience as human consciousness. This is our most compelling evidence of brain plasticity. We ask ourselves: How does the mind (or the brain) become capable of contemplating itself? How are we able to conceive of ourselves as beings with a unique consciousness who learn, remember, and forget, rather than as masses of protoplasm, emitting chemical signals? These are questions yet to be answered by neuroscience.

Historical Background

The term *plasticity* may be thought of as a relatively recent addition to the lexicon of neuroscience, but, as has so often been the case, the term was first introduced by William James (1842–1910), in his book *Principles of Psychology* (1890). Even then, the concept of plasticity reprised a time-worn theme. The notion was implicit in the epistemology of the early Greek philosophers, e.g., Anaxagoras (500–428 B.C.) and, later, Aristotle (384–322 B.C.), the latter of whom first proposed that we come to *know* through a process of change that occurs as the result of sensory experience. Aristotle's four principles of association, as set forth in *De Memoria et Reminiscentia*, continued as the foundation for scientific views of learning and memory for two millennia. It may be instructive to briefly consider them:

1. Contiguity. Things or events that occur close to each other in space or time tend to become linked together in the mind. If you think of a dog, you may think of another domestic animal like a cat; if you think about the action of walking the dog, you may then think of throwing a ball to that dog.

2. Frequency. The more often two things or events are linked, the more powerful will be that association. If you use cream with your coffee every day, the association between coffee and cream will be strong.

3. Similarity. If two things are similar, the thought of one will tend to trigger the thought of the other. If you think of a Porsche sports car, it is easier to think of a Ferrari. If you think about speaking in public, you may also find yourself thinking about acting or singing in public.

4. Contrast. Seeing or recalling an object or event may also trigger the recollection of something completely opposite. If you think of a tall person you may also think of a short person. If you are thinking about winter, you may find yourself thinking about spring as well.

The influence of Aristotle extended well beyond the threshold of modern psychological science. The British empiricist Thomas Hobbes (1588–1679), like Aristotle, believed that the contents of the mind were related to sensory experience, and in his *Human Nature* (1650) proposed the doctrine of *association* that was dependent on the *coherence* of past ideas. Four decades later, John Locke (1632–1704), in his *Essay Concerning Human Understanding* (1690), proposed (following Aristotle) that the human mind was a *tabula rasa* (literally, an "erased slate," but now usually translated as a "blank slate" or "white paper"), which accumulated all knowledge through sensory experience. Locke's irrefutable support for his theory was the fact that a person could have knowledge at one moment that was not present at any prior moment, and that lawful predictions could be generated regarding the conditions under which such knowledge had come to be learned. To learn, said Locke, we must record our experiences on the *tabula rasa*.

Let us suppose the mind to be, as we say, white paper, void of all characters, without any ideas; How comes it to be furnished? Whence comes it by that vast store, which the busy and boundless fancy of man has painted on it with an almost endless variety? Whence has it all the material of reason and knowledge? To this I answer, in one word, from experience. In that all our knowledge is founded and from that it ultimately derives itself. (*Essay Concerning Human Understanding*, 1690)

Locke's successors, who came to be known as the "British Associationists"—George Berkeley (1685–1753), David Hartley (1705–1757), David Hume (1711–1776), and James Mill (1773–1836)—augmented his (and Aristotle's) laws of association with the law of cause and effect, the distinction between simultaneous and successive associations, and the law of repetition. To this day, none of these laws have lost their relevance for an understanding of learning and memory. An especially important contribution came from John Stuart Mill (1806–1873), who pointed out that *contiguity* depended on the *frequency* of concurrences, and thereby named *frequency* as a separate law. Mill also posited *intensity* as a third law of association. In his *Logic of the moral sciences*, in 1843, he wrote:

> *It is obvious that the complex laws of thought and feeling not only may, but must be generated from those simple laws [of association]. When impressions have so often been experienced in conjunction, so that each of them calls up readily and instantaneously the ideas of the whole, these ideas sometimes melt and coalesce into one another. When many impressions or ideas are operating in the mind together, there sometimes takes place a process that is similar to chemical combination.*

As we shall see in subsequent sections, frequency and intensity remain pillars of current learning and memory theories.

When Wilhelm Wundt (1832–1920) established the first psychological laboratory, at Leipzig, in 1879, his laws of association reflected the influence of Aristotle and the British Associationists. Wundt distinguished several types of association. First, there was *fusion*, which involved a blending of the elements of sensation with a consequent loss of independence among them and a dominance of one element over the others. Secondly there was *assimilation*, by similarity or by contrast, such as found in the optical illusions. Third, there were the *complications*, which accounted for associations between different sensory departments. As influential as Wundt may have been for the science of psychology, his thoughts on memory were soon to be eclipsed by those of another German psychologist, Hermann Ebbinghaus (1850–1909).

Six years after Wundt founded his laboratory, Ebbinghaus published the results of a remarkable series of experiments on human memory. His goal was that of identifying the factors determining why we remember some things and forget others. In doing so, he was the first person to apply the scientific method to the problem. In order to measure the manner in which memory traces were established, Ebbinghaus determined that he had to have material to be recalled that was *uniformly unassociated*. To accomplish this, he selected two consonants and a vowel, a *trigram*, at random and put them together (e.g., "zat," "bok," "sud"). He thus found himself in possession of about 2,300 *nonsense syllables* that could be assembled into lists for learning. A list of nonsense syllables was much more homogeneous than a list of words, the latter having the drawbacks of varying lengths and linguistic meanings, so that between-word associations of unknown degree had been already formed.

For Ebbinghaus, the lists of nonsense syllables were his only experimental materials. He was his sole research subject! He measured the number of exposures, or trials that it took him to master a list, typically to a criterion of two successive errorless repetitions and how much he retained after an interposed time period, which he called *savings*. In 1885, he completed his first publication, an epic report of this work under the title *Ueber das Gedachtnis*. Therein was contained the results of his many experiments, which included: 1) systematically varying the duration of the learning process to determine the most effective route towards mastery of the material to be learned; 2) testing retention of a list as a function of differing numbers of repetitions; 3) determining the relationship of elapsed time from learning to forgetting material once learned (the famous *forgetting curve*); and, 4) assessing the strength of direct and remote, as well as forward and backward, associations within a given set of materials. For example, he varied the number of his exposures to a given list of syllables, and the amount of time that lapsed between his mastery of the list and testing his recall, to see how much memory was saved, as a function of the original learning conditions. He typically learned twelve nonsense syllables to criterion and then tried to see how many relearning trials he needed to reach the same criterion after one to six days. Using these simple methods, Ebbinghaus discovered many of the basic characteristics of learning and memory. Indeed, to this day his work is cited in virtually every introductory psychology textbook, and most of the laws he discovered are relevant to the *Brainfit* exercises.

As mentioned earlier, by the time Ebbinghaus began his work, the laws of association had gradually converged upon frequency as the primary condition of learning, but it was Ebbinghaus who first experimentally validated the importance of frequency. In working out the parameters relevant to the measurement of learning and memory, he identified *frequency of repetition* as the essential condition, that is, his "mastery" of a list was a function of the number of times he repeated the list while learning it. Typical Ebbinghaus learning and forgetting curves are shown in Figures 1 and 2, on the next page.

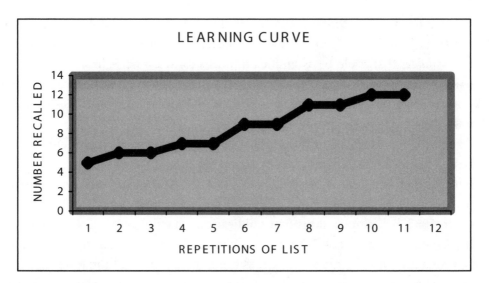

Figure 1. Illustration, adapted from Ebbinghaus' data, showing the number of repetitions necessary for him to recall a list of 12 nonsense syllables to a "mastery" criterion of error-less repetition on two successive trials.

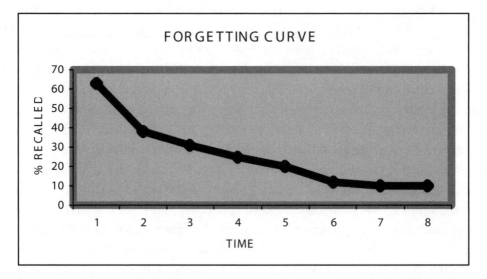

Figure 2. Illustration, adapted from Ebbinghaus' data, showing the percent recall of a list of 12 nonsense syllables as a function of time from initial mastery. Here his retention curve indicates that he retained only 63 percent of the learned information after 20 minutes, 38 percent after 1 day, 31 percent after 2 days, and 25 percent after 31 days, and so forth.

Appendix

In addition to the effects of repetition on initial learning and the effects of time on memory decay, Ebbinghaus is remembered for demonstrating several other important lawful relationships related to learning and memory. Among these were: 1) *the total time hypothesis*; 2) *the principle of distributed practice*; 3) *the overlearning effect*; and 4) *the serial position effect*. The most intuitively sensible of these, the total time hypothesis, stated that the amount learned is a direct function of the time devoted to learning. Thus, if Ebbinghaus studied a list for sixty minutes he learned it twice as well than if he only studied it for thirty minutes (assuming, of course, that he spent all of the study time actually trying to learn the list).

The principle of distributed practice was not quite as evident from non-experimental evidence. It holds that it is better to spread out study over time, rather than massing it together in one session. For example, Ebbinghaus found that he learned more by studying material ten minutes per day for six days than by studying it for sixty minutes in a single day. In demonstrating the distributed practice principle, Ebbinghaus reported an experiment showing that after he went through sixty-eight repetitions of twelve nonsense syllables in one day, the next day the material required seven repetitions to be relearned. But when he spaced thirty-eight repetitions across three days, he required only six repetitions on the fourth day for the list to be learned. In a rather remarkable extension of this work, Ebbinghaus decided to learn some stanzas from the poetry of Byron by massed learning and then relearn them *after twenty-two years*! There was a saving of 7 percent. He contrasted this learning with that of other stanzas of the same poem, learned to the same criterion (one perfect repetition) over four consecutive days. After the same twenty-two-year period, Ebbinghaus could remember 20 percent of these memorized stanzas, demonstrating the superiority of distributed practice.

Ebbinghaus was the first to discover the relation between the serial position of an item (its place in the list) and his ability to recall it. Items near the beginning of the list were easier to recall than those in the middle (the *primacy effect*). Those near the end of the list were also easier to recall than those in the middle (the *recency effect).* However, some fifty years after Ebbinghaus published *Ueber das Gedachtnis*, it was shown that the disadvantage in remembering a middle-list item could be reduced or eliminated by making the item *distinctive*, so that it stood out from the other middle-list items. For example, the item could be printed in red when the rest of the items were printed in black. The contrasting color would draw attention to the item, and it received more processing. Consequently, it was memorized more easily than its mere serial position would dictate. In addition, items on either side of the distinctive item were shown to also be more likely to be remembered that would otherwise have been the case.

The improved memory for distinctive items in the middle of a list is known as the Von Restorff effect, after its discoverer, Hedwig Von Restorff (1906–1962), who published her results in 1933. In the typical Von Restorff experiment, there might be a list of seven items and the subject's task would be to recall the items in their original order. In the control condition, a list such as RMSKQLF might be used, while in the experimental condition, a list such as RMS4QLF might be used. The typical finding was that the subjects would be more likely to recall the digit 4 than the letter *K*. This effect is also known as the *isolation effect* because the 4 is isolated in the sense that it is the only digit in the set.

During the same decade that *Ueber das Gedachtnis* was published two other noteworthy treatises on memory appeared: in Russia, Sergei Korsakoff's article on disturbances of memory associated with alcoholism (1889), and, in America, the aforementioned William James' *Principles of Psychology* (1890).

Korsakoff's observations of patients with dementia induced by alcoholism (now called "Korsakoff's syndrome") was important because it showed that the disease was characterized by an inability to remember, over time, information that seemed to have been initially learned. In fact, when the information was again presented to the patients, they acted as if they were quite unfamiliar with it—"zero savings," in Ebbinghaus' terms. Korsakoff's observations were important precursors to what later became known as *consolidation theory*, the notion that, over time, memory traces are transferred from short-term storage areas of the brain to long-term storage areas from whence they must then be retrieved. Consolidation theory will be discussed in greater detail below, as it is important evidence of *ongoing plasticity* following initial learning in that some memories must eventually become stored in a manner that makes them more resistant to decay. Korsakoff's patients seemed to lack the capability of moving their immediate experiences to a long-term memory bank and/or retrieving the stored memories.

William James, who introduced the term *plasticity* in his *Principles,* explained that the mind is *cumulative,* and not *recurrent.* Consider, for example, his simple but profound observation: "No state once gone can recur and be identical with what was before." He pointed out that objects can recur, but not sensations or thoughts. James believed that when the stimulus-object comes again it finds a "different" mind, and together the old object and the new mind yield a brand-new conscious state. It was James who distinguished between two kinds of memory, short term and long term. It was also James who noted that one of the most essential of all mental functions is that of forgetting. Consider the inefficiency of the alternative: remembering everything (or forgetting nothing)!

The empirical extension of James' theories of knowledge was left to Edward Lee Thorndike (1874–1949), who had been inspired by courses he had taken from James at Harvard. Thorndike's results on learning in cats, using puzzle boxes, were demonstrated through learning curves, which illustrated the length of time it took for the animal to get out of the box on the first trial, on the second trial, third trial, and so forth.

Thorndike believed in a simple trial-and-error explanation of learning. He thought that quite by chance an animal would perform an action such as lifting a latch, which freed it from the box. When the animal found itself in the same position again it was more likely to perform the same action again. The reward of being freed from the box somehow strengthened an association between a stimulus, being in a certain position in the box, and an appropriate action. Thorndike believed that reward acted to strengthen *stimulus-response (S-R) associations*. He believed that the animal learned to solve the puzzle-box not by reflecting on possible actions that might be taken, and thereby insightfully "puzzling" its way out of the box, but by a quite mechanical development of *chains of actions,* originally made by chance. Thorndike formalized this notion into the "law" for which he remains famous—the law of effect. In full, it reads:

> *Of several responses made to the same situation, those which are accompanied or closely followed by satisfaction to the animal will, other things being equal, be more firmly connected with the situation, so that, when it recurs, they will be more likely to recur; those which are accompanied or closely followed by discomfort to the animal will, other things being equal, have their connections to the situation weakened, so that, when it recurs, they will be less likely to occur. The greater the satisfaction or discomfort, the greater the strengthening or weakening of the bond. (Animal Intelligence: An Experimental Study of the Associative Process in Animals, 1898)*

Thorndike maintained that two other factors were involved in strengthening associations, namely, 1) that associations are *strengthened by use and weakened with disuse*, and 2) that some behaviors are *instinctual*. In combination with the law of effect, these three principles could explain all of human behavior, which Thorndike viewed as the development of myriads of S-R associations. He wrote that the success of a correct movement caused that movement to be *impressed*, or to be learned. The success was the effect of the movement, and *stamped in* the movement. Thorndike wrote that the traces of the past were *stamped in* so that the past might thereafter more readily recur. He identified success with *satisfaction*. He thought that this new principle, satisfaction, operated in addition to frequency and repetition, or, as he called it, *exercise*. From Ebbinghaus, frequency had become the primary law of association. Now, Thorndike had two: *exercise* (his term for frequency); and *effect* (or reward).

Memory and Changes in the Higher Central Nervous System

The modern day neuroscientist views memory and learning as evidence of neural plasticity—more or less permanent changes in brain function that take place as the result of experience. But this notion is not unique to the twentieth or twenty-first centuries. Indeed, one of the earliest conceptualizations of the biological basis of memory may be found in the writings of Rene Descartes (1596–1650):

> *When the mind wills to recall something, this volition causes the little gland* [i.e., the pineal gland], *by inclining successively to different sides, to impel the animal spirits toward different parts of the brain, until they come upon that part where the traces are left of the thing which it wished to remember: for these traces are nothing else than the circumstance that the pores of the brain, through which the spirits have already taken their course on presentation of the object, have thereby acquired a greater facility than the rest to be opened again the same way by the spirits which come to them so that these spirits coming upon the pores enter therein more readily than into the others.* (*Trait de L'homme*, 1662).

By 1890, when James published his *Principles,* there was no dispute that learning and memory reflected neural activity that somehow changed over time, but the neural mechanisms underlying that change were still highly speculative. Consider, for example, Thorndike's formulation:

> *Connections between neurons are strengthened every time they are used with indifferent or pleasurable results, and weakened every time they are used with resultant discomfort. The line of least resistance [to the transmission of the nerve impulse] is, other things being equal, that resulting in the greatest satisfaction to the animal.* (*The Elements of Psychology*, 1905)

The neuroanatomists and neurophysiologists of the late nineteenth century assumed the central nervous system to be a continuous network, "hard-wired," as it were, from the brain (the so-called reticular theory). Yet, it was hard to reconcile this conceptualization of nervous system wiring with evidence from contemporaneous learning experiments (e.g., how frequency or intensity strengthened associations).

The Founders of Neural Plasticity

RAMON Y CAJAL

It was only with the elegant and imaginative experiments of the great Spanish neuroanatomist, Santiago Ramon y Cajal (1852–1934) that a plausible physical substrate for behavioral plasticity—sufficient to support existing data from learning and memory experiments—finally emerged. Cajal's observations, largely unappreciated at the time or their publication, led to a new interpretation of neuronal activity: the *Neuron Doctrine*. For Cajal, the neuron, or nerve cell, was the primary anatomical, physiological, and metabolic unit of the nervous system. No one before Cajal had actually visualized a nerve cell in all of its richness of structure, nor had anyone determined that each nerve cell was an independent structure. In 1889, Cajal first showed his drawings, derived from microscopic views of brain slices that were stained to reveal the architecture of the nerve cells, to the German Anatomical Society.

Cajal's innovative staining technique revealed that each nerve cell stood out independently against a background of staggering complexity. More striking for the scientific world of the time was Cajal's demonstration that no matter how many times the tiny fibers of one nerve cell *came close* to those of another there was clearly no physical connection between cells. The basic unit of brain activity—the neuron—was anatomically isolated! (Ramon y Cajal, 1909, 1911). To this day, Cajal's meticulous drawings are a defining fixture of virtually all neuroscience texts.

But, as theories of memory and learning emerged in the early twentieth century, not much notice seems to have been given to the Cajal's neuron theory. Indeed, in the fifty years following Cajal's revelations to the German Anatomical Society, the S-R theorists held sway, continuing to naively assume some form of hard-wired higher nervous system in which existing bonds were strengthened or weakened as the result of experience. As mentioned earlier, one of the major contributors to this movement was the prolific Thorndike. Great attention was paid to the laws that permitted prediction of behavioral outcomes from the experimental conditions imposed, with the nervous system treated as a "black box."

KARL LASHLEY

One notable exception to the strict S-R orientation of the early twentieth century was found in the work of Karl Lashley (1890–1958), considered the father of the science of neuropsychology. Lashley's imaginative experiments with brain-lesioned animals provided a wealth of evidence regarding the neural basis of learning. His theories of mass action and equipotentiality have continued to provoke experimentation for three quarters of a century, and, today, some of his interpretations are still considered necessary in explaining phenomena such as the recovery of function after brain injury. However, in perhaps his most famous paper, Lashley (1950) despaired of ever locating the *memory trace*:

> *I sometimes feel, in reviewing the evidence on the localization of the memory trace, that the necessary conclusion is that learning just is not possible. It is difficult to conceive of a mechanism which can satisfy the conditions set for it. Nevertheless, in spite of such evidence against it, learning does sometimes occur. (In Search of the Engram, 1950)*

Lashley pointed out a number of critical problems for simple S-R interpretations of phenomena such as learning and memory. In his studies of recovery of function, he showed that monkeys who were trained to open latch boxes would apparently lose the habit for eight to twelve weeks following a brain injury, but then regain their ability *without practice*. He was able to demonstrate functional equivalence—that is, that a learned motor act was not necessarily performed by a single set of neuromuscular connections—an animal unable to walk would even roll down the correct pathway in a maze! And, of considerable importance in our understanding of material that follows this introduction, Lashley showed that memory was highly contextual. By way of example: an animal that learned an association between a particular triangle and a food reward would not to go to the same triangle when it was rotated fifteen or more degrees; an animal that learned to go to the triangle B, which was larger than triangle A, would go automatically go to triangle C, which was larger than triangle B, even though B had been previously associated with the reward. With experiments such as these, Lashley demonstrated that memory was dynamic, and not static. These were formidable problems for a simplistic S-R theory.

Lashley also demonstrated that there were different kinds of memory, each type supported by a somewhat different set of brain mechanisms. He was especially interested in the *serial timing* of memories—how they were ordered in the context of an individual's past history. For example, one may remember all of the notes that comprise Beethoven's *Moonlight Sonata*, but how are they a) recorded in memory so that the precise sequence of their occurrence is maintained, and b) retrieved from memory in precisely the correct sequence so that when the notes are played again, they are recognized as the *Moonlight Sonata*? S-R connectionist theories were hard pressed to account for the problem of serial memory and serial memory retrieval posed by Lashley.

DONALD HEBB

As Lashley (no doubt tongue-in-cheek) was giving up his search for the memory engram, a second-generation neuropsychologist, Donald Hebb (1904–1985), was publishing a theoretical bombshell that continues to guide investigations into the neural basis of learning and memory into the twenty-first century. Before Hebb's emergence on the scene, Cajal's stunning revelations, enshrined by the neuranatomical world for their artistic elegance and precision, had not fulfilled their latent promise for a greater understanding of learning and memory processes. Hebb (1949), reflecting on the importance of Cajal's discoveries, wrote:

> *One is accustomed to thinking of the nerve cell as a static structure (as it is after being fixed and stained), and of growth as a very slow process. Yet it may be recalled that Cajal (among others) conjectured that the change at the synapse in learning is an ameboid outgrowth of the cell, which might need very little time for it occurrences. Cajal's proposal has been disregarded by psychologists in discussions of learning. Presumably, this is partly because the whole theory of synaptic connections and resistances fell into disrepute some time ago. But it has been seen that modern neurophysiology makes it possible to repose this entire question, and so Cajal's idea cannot be at once dismissed as fantastic.* (The Organization of Behavior, 1949)

Hebb's magnum opus, *The Organization of Behavior* (1949), appeared six decades after Cajal's presentation to the German Academy. Within a few years of its publication, it was universally acknowledged that what Hebb was proposing had opened a new chapter in our understanding of the relationship of brain activity to memory, learning, and other mental functions. Like many before him, Hebb assumed that the wiring diagram of the brain was altered by experience, but he started with an inquiry into how the initial short term storage of individual memories, a necessary first step in the process, might take place. Here, the memory trace was seen as a function of a pattern of neural activity, independent of any structural changes. His assumption, in brief, was that a growth process accompanied activity at the synapse, the cleft between one nerve cell and another. Hebb suggested that persistent synaptic activity might render the space between the nerve cells more readily traversed.

Hebb proposed that repeated stimulation of specific receptors, that is, anatomical areas on the nerve cells that received information from other nerve cells, would lead slowly to the formation of an assembly of nerve cells that could act briefly as a closed loop after stimulation had ceased. This prolonged the time during which the structural changes that accompany learning might occur. In considering and answering to one of the thorniest of the problems that had been posed by Lashley, Hebb supposed that there could be a memory trace that was wholly a function of a pattern of neural activity, independent of any structural changes.

> There are memories which are instantaneously established, and as evanescent as they are immediate. In the repetition of digits, for example, an interval of a few seconds is enough to prevent any interference from one series on the next. Also, some memories are both instantaneously established and permanent. To account for the change, some structural change seems necessary, but a structural growth presumably could require an appreciable time. If some way can be found of supposing that a reverberatory trace might cooperate with the structural change, and carry the memory until the growth change is made, we would be able to recognize the theoretical value of the trace which is an activity only, without having to ascribe all memory to it. (*The Organization of Behavior*, 1949)

Hebb speculated that the persistence or repetition of a *reverberatory activity* (or a temporary trace of a pattern of neural signals) tended to induce lasting cellular changes that added to the stability of a circuit. When a nerve fiber transmitting information from nerve cell A was near enough to excite nerve cell B, and repeatedly or persistently took part in firing it, some growth process or metabolic change took place in one or both cells such that As effectiveness, as one of the cells firing B, was increased. Hebb imagined that these *cell assemblies* became organized into larger structures, called *phase sequences*, which were the substrate for more complex concepts. Like Cajal, Hebb believed that the most probable way in which one cell became more capable of firing another was that synaptic knobs, anatomical outgrowths that Cajal had first visualized, developed and increased the area of contact between one nerve cell and another. While there was still, at that time, no direct evidence that this was so, Hebb thought that the postulated change was probably metabolic, affecting the rhythm of a cell and its threshold for firing; but, he considered that it was possible that there were both metabolic and structural changes. In this way, any two cells or system of cells that were repeatedly active at the same time would tend to become associated.

Hebb went on to further hypothesize that a nerve cell could only be fired by the simultaneous activity of two or more incoming fibers, and that sets of nerve fibers were arranged in closed, potentially self-exciting relationships. Hebb imagined that, rather than acting as a closed loop, this reverberatory activity took place in a three-dimensional lattice within the brain, with connections possible from any one intersection to any other. The specificity of such an assembly of cells to a particular excitation depended on *convergence*. The two converging cells need not have any simple anatomical or physiological relationship to one another, only to the cell upon which they were converging.

Hebb's concept of complex cell assemblies dealt with another of Lashley's criteria—a system inherently involving the capacity for *equipotentiality*, that is, the presence of alternate pathways for a particular function, each having the same potential for adaptively responding, so that brain damage might remove some pathways without preventing the system as a whole from functioning. We might consider this the equivalent of modern-day back up computers on spacecraft, or redundant operators built into robotic systems. Hebb thought that if the system had been long established, with well-developed synaptic knobs, it might decrease the number of fibers that must be active at once to traverse a synapse. However, in a simplified or automatic system redundancy might be lost. For example, recovery of speech function after brain injury occurs more readily in children than adults, presumably because in childhood a wider variety of connections remain available for the task.

Hebb concluded that, to the extent that anatomical and physiological observations established the possibility of reverberatory after effects of sensory events, such a process would become the physiological basis of memory.

Modern Evidence of Plasticity

Cajal, Lashley, and Hebb set the stage for a neuroscience that could scarcely have been imagined by Aristotle. It would go well beyond the scope of this introduction to enumerate the countless experiments in which the hypotheses generated by these three giants have now been confirmed. But, in the fifty-five years since Hebb's *The Organization* first appeared, there have been many memorable demonstrations of the scope and extent of neural plasticity. With human memory tending to be selective, every neuroscientist has his or her own list of favorites. Those that come to mind at present are given below.

THE WORMRUNNERS (1955)

In 1955, Robert Thompson, who had worked with Lashley at the Yerkes Laboratory, and his fellow University of Texas graduate student, James McConnell, conceived a simple but imaginative experiment. In their apartment sink, they trained planaria, small flatworms (that they scooped from a pond on the Texas campus), to swim from one side of a shallow pan to the other when a light signal was given, in order to avoid receiving an electric shock. After the flatworms had learned the habit, they were cut in half, horizontally, so that one half had the head and the other half had the tail. When each of the two halves regenerated into a whole worm, as will happen with planaria, both of the regenerated animals continued to remember to avoid the shock! This simple experiment was laden with implications for neural plasticity. How could the memory for this habit be retained in the head, which contained the animal's primitive brain, as well as the tail, which did not? Later, McConnell (1962) trained other planaria, ground them up, and fed them to untrained flatworms, which were then found to "know" to avoid the shock. Some plastic process had happened to the animal in the course of its learning that seemed to have pervaded every cell in its body. These were among the first demonstration of a memory trace that was seemingly the result of *chemically mediated plasticity*. Studies of learning and memory in flatworms became so ubiquitous that McConnell and his colleagues later began publishing them in their own journal, aptly entitled: *The Wormrunner's Digest*.

MEMORY CONSOLIDATION (1957)

ECS. Electroconvulsive shock (ECS) was introduced as a treatment for psychiatric illness in the early 1940s. Following ECS, which induced the equivalent of an epileptic grand mal seizure and periodic loss of consciousness, the patients were found to have *retroactive amnesia,* that is, a loss of memory that extended back some time before the shock was given, but no loss of memory for earlier life events. In 1957, Robert Thompson and his colleagues at Southeast Louisiana State Hospital, having observed this effect in human patients, experimentally repeated the process in animals. They found that the shorter the time interval between learning and the onset of shock, the more likely it became that memory for the learned habit would be obliterated. Memories for habits learned well before the onset of shock were not affected. These findings were consistent with the evidence from studies of neurological patients who had experienced traumatic brain injury with resultant amnesia—short-term memories were more fragile than long term (Thompson, 1957a, 1957b, Thompson & Pennington, 1957).

The ECS experiments focused on the process of consolidation, a phenomenon that could be inferred from amnesias, but not systematically investigated to any extent before ECS became available as an investigatory tool. Not only ECS, but the effects of minor concussions, alcohol or drug-induced blackouts, and the fragility of information learned while "cramming" for an examination are all phenomena that support consolidation theory. Consolidation of a memory may occur within a relatively short time frame, but there is usually a period of time during which the memory remains in a fragile state. If memories could be maintained in some fashion over a given time frame, perhaps in reverberating circuits as suggested by Hebb, consolidation seemed to occur, and the memory became more resistant to extinction. For many years, the exact nature of these permanent, or consolidated, changes remained elusive.

ENRICHED ENVIRONMENTS (1961)

Perhaps the most dramatic evidence of brain plasticity came from a series of ingenious studies that took place at the University of California, Berkeley, in the 1960s. Mark Rosenzweig, David Krech, Marian Diamond, and their colleagues showed that experience, more precisely the *quality of experience,* does, in fact, affect a) brain anatomy, b) brain chemistry, and c) brain electrical activity. Instead of training animals to remember certain tasks and then analyzing their brains, Krech and his associates decided to raise some animals in an enriched environment, in which opportunities existed for enhanced informal learning, while their littermates were confined to standard laboratory cages. At maturity, the brains of both groups of animals were analyzed, and a number of interesting findings obtained. First, the animals from the enriched environment had more of the brain chemical acetylcholine (AChE) present (Rosenzweig, Krech & Bennet, 1961). Even a single training experience could result in neurochemical changes in the brain (Rosenzweig, Krech, Bennett, & Diamond, 1962). Furthermore, the enriched animals had thicker cerebral cortexes and heavier brains (Diamond, Krech & Rozenzweig, 1964). It was also found that the number of glial cells in the brain, that is, cells that supply metabolic support for the neurons, seemed to increase as the result of environmental enrichment (Diamond, Law, Rhodes, Lindner, Rozenzweig, Krech, & Bennett, 1966).

In the 1970s, eighty years after Cajal had suggested to the German Academy that experience might result in the growth of dendrites (fiber branches emanating from nerve cells that receive information from other nerve cells), it was shown that an enriched environment did indeed result in more dendrites on nerve cells (Greenough & Volkmar, 1973). The nerve cells of animals from enriched environments did not seem to send their branches any farther but rather tended to fill up the allotted space within the brain with more branches, providing strong evidence in support of Cajal's earlier conjecture.

NEURAL SPROUTING AND CELL DEATH (1976)

Sprouting. Today, few neuroscientists would contradict the premise that learning and memory are manifestations of an ever-changing brain capable of growing new circuitry rather than a static structure that simply modifies the strength of its embryologically defined wiring patterns. The gross anatomy of the brain may not appear to change, but the synaptic connections between brain cells are exceedingly plastic. These synaptic junctions have the capacity to support learning and memory. Dendrites show a capacity for growth and change far in excess of anything previously imagined, even by Hebb or Cajal, and adjustments in dendritic architecture would seem to be the basis for learning and memory.

In 1976, neuroscientists Gary Lynch and Carl Cotman, of the Department of Psychobiology at the University of California, Irvine, demonstrated that isolating a brain section from input from other sections caused shrinkage of that structure but increases in density in the population of remaining intact terminals, i.e., the points on the nerve cells that to receive input from other nerve cells. They found that removal of one input could increase the density of remaining inputs without requiring any growth response by those remaining fibers and terminals. This phenomenon, shown by electron microscopic studies of brain tissue, is usually cited as evidence of neural sprouting—providing yet another mechanism of plasticity. Such plasticity did not require growth of the nerve fiber, lengthwise, but could be explained by a simpler process; namely, formation of new contacts between existing terminals and the denervated dendrites.

Cell death. In 1951, another form of plasticity was first reported by the distinguished Cambridge physiologist Alfred Glucksmann. Many cells, including nerve cells, are actively programmed to commit suicide in a natural process called apoptosis. This is different from the death of nerve cells due to trauma, infection, or poisoning, which is accompanied by an inflammatory response that literally blows up the cells. Apoptosis by contrast, causes cells to shrink or fall away, somewhat akin to the manner in which petals fall off a flower. This programmed cell death is a natural developmental process, apparently mediated by inborn genetic programs. One seeming benefit of apoptosis is that it will destroy cells that may have come to contain faulty genetic material, serving to protect the surrounding healthy neurons (Glucksmann,1951).

Apoptosis is a natural part of development of the immature central nervous system. There is a built-in redundancy of neurons early in development. These neurons compete vigorously to connect with other neurons, and also for nutrients to fuel the process. Normally, extra neurons are available in a brain bank until the wiring of the brain is completed, and then the extras neurons are discarded by apoptosis. There is survival of the fittest because about 50 percent of neurons will normally die before birth.

In the late 1970s, Peter Huttenlocher of the University of Chicago conducted research in which he counted synapses in samples of human brain tissue to determine how the number and density of synaptic connections might change over the life spans. Huttenlocher found that, starting a few months after birth and continuing until age three, various parts of the brain formed synapses very rapidly. This early, exuberant synaptic growth resulted in synaptic densities in children's brains that were much higher than the densities in adult brains. In humans, synaptic densities appear to remain at these elevated levels until puberty, when some mechanism that is apparently under genetic control causes synapses to be eliminated, reducing them to the lower adult levels. As the child grows, the brain selectively strengthens or "prunes" connections based on experience. Failure to eliminate excess neurons would be akin to having unneeded or redundant circuits on a computer chip (Huttenlocher, 1979).

Thus, the folk wisdom that a loss of brain cells is necessarily accompanied by a loss of adaptive capacity is confuted by an extensive literature documenting the benefits of programmed cell death. Considering the billions of brain cells affected by programmed cell death, both before and after birth, apoptosis qualifies as perhaps the most extensive evidence of neural plasticity.

VIEWING PLASTICITY IN ACTION (1973)

The most graphic evidence of brain plasticity has come from brain imaging studies. In earlier imaging studies, the brain was visualized by constructing images derived from computerized analysis of brain electrical activity, using the electroencephalograph (EEG), or by computerized tomography (CT), which takes X-rays of the brain in multiple slices.

A remarkable breakthrough in imaging took place in 1973, when positron emission tomography (PET) was introduced by Michael Phelps, at Washington University in St. Louis. The PET image was developed through administration of a radioactive tracer (a radioactive compound whose activity, represented by the movement of the emitted *positrons*, are detectable by a scanner), along with a natural body compound. For example, the radioactive tracer in many brain studies is fluorodeoxyglucose (FDG), which combines the natural body compound, glucose, with the radioisotope Fluorine-18.

Brain cells at work use glucose as their fuel. Consequently, through measuring the activity of the emitted positrons, the neuroscientist is able to identify brain activity of conscious, alert subjects, showing detailed biochemical changes that occur with various experiences. In areas where there is high brain activity, large amounts of FDG are consumed; in areas where there is less active brain activity, there is less absorption of FDG. Subsequent studies from the Neuroimaging Laboratory at the Washington University School of Medicine showed that different parts of the brain are activated when performing different mental tasks such as hearing, reading, talking, and thinking. Much of this work was summarized in the book, *Images of Mind*, by Michael Posner and Marcus Raichle (1994).

The value of PET for studying normal brain function was highlighted by other experiments. In the preceding section, we learned about programmed cell death and neural pruning. In a seminal article in the 1987 *Annals of Neurology*, Harry Chugani, professor of pediatrics, neurology and radiology, at Wayne State University in Detroit, along with Michael Phelps and John Mazziotta, reported results of PET scans on children ranging in age from five days to fifteen years. One of the major findings was that metabolic levels reached adult values when children were approximately two years old and continued to increase, reaching rates twice the adult level by age three or four Resting glucose uptake remained at this elevated level until the children were around nine years old. At age nine, the rates of brain glucose metabolism started to decline and stabilized at adult values by the end of the teenage years. The peak period for metabolic activity in the brain that lasted from roughly age three to ten years.

This work converged on Huttenlocher's evidence, cited in the previous section, in which the information regarding developmental plasticity had been gained by counting synapses in human brain tissue. Now, with the use of PET, there was evidence suggesting that maintaining all of these synapses in the childhood years probably accounted for most of the glucose consumed by the brain. As the density and number of synapses waxed and waned so too did the rate of brain-glucose metabolism.

PET scanning has some disadvantages, including the necessity for subjects to take in radioactive isotopes. More importantly, PET scans usually show the results of activity that has taken place over an extended time frame. An alternate technique, functional magnetic resonance imaging (fMRI) has the advantage of greater temporal resolution, allowing for "event-based" experiments. We've all had the experience of being unable to recall from memory something that we're certain we know and will remember some time later, a phenomenon that has been called the *feeling of knowing* phenomenon. Anat Maril and colleagues of the Department of Psychology at Harvard University conducted an ingenious analysis of the feeling of knowing phenomenon, using fMRI. A pattern of neural activation in the frontal lobes was associated with both successful remembering as well as the feeling of knowing; on the other hand, less activity was seen in this same area when the subject did not know the item at all (Maril, Simons, Mitchell, Schwartz & Schacter, 2003).

Neuroscientist John Gabrieli, of Stanford University, and his colleagues have been using fMRI to indicate how we learn to read. In one study, adult subjects were given mirror-reversed text to read, and predictably, they had trouble with letters like *b* and *d*. During the time they were attempting to master this process, an area called the *right parietal cortex* was shown to be active. After the mirror-reading task was mastered, the *left temporal cortex*, the classic language processing area of the brain, was active, just as it would have been if the subjects had been reading normal text—visual evidence of the plasticity that has occurred when we finally master a complex and confusing task (Poldrack & Gabrieli, 2001). In another dramatic experiment by the Gabrieli group, published in 2003 in the prestigious *Proceedings of the National academy of Sciences,* eight to twelve-year-old dyslexic children were trained using the Fast ForWord language software. At the conclusion of training, the program was associated with significant improvement in oral language and reading performance; further, fMRI imaging showed increased activity in brain areas involved in language processing (Temple, Poldrack, Deutsch, Miller, Tallal, Merzinich & Gabrieli, 2003). Experiments such as these show that with fMRI we not only see the location of the greatest amount of mental processing but the dynamic interplay of different brain networks as the task is progressively learned—not only the *where* but the *when* of plasticity.

Appendix

Brainfit and Neural Darwinism

If there were a single theory capable of encompassing most of what we now know about neural plasticity, a good candidate might be that proposed by Nobel Laureate Gerald Edelman, as outlined in his 1987 book *Neural Darwinism*. Edelman's theory of neuronal group selection answers the questions of how connections are made between neurons that then come to be assembled into large groups. A key concept of Edelman's theory is that the brain operates as a selective system. For Edelman, there is no master plan for the architecture of the brain, and there is no central management system. The brain is organized into groups of neurons during its embryonic stage, and once formed into groups, the interconnected neurons function as units (no neuron is able to operate on its own). Edelman's theory makes three fundamental claims for these units:

1. The diversity of neuronal groups occurs because of the random and highly variable manner of connecting neurons to each other in the development stage. In the absence of a master plan, connections just happen by self-selection. The "repertoire," or structured collection of such groups, is such that no two persons are ever likely to have identical connections between brain regions.

2. Once a child is born and begins to behave in its new environment, some of the connections between neuronal groups are strengthened and some are weakened. The result is a new combination of groups from the primary repertoire, now associated with signals from the outside world. These new formations create a set of groups called the "secondary repertoire" that is now prepared to respond to future adaptive challenges.

3. Eventually the groups in this secondary repertoire are called into action. When the groups are re-entered into memory, they are modified by how they have been used. Those groups that lead behavior into results that are satisfying are "stamped into" our nervous system, while those resulting in pain or discomfort are erased (much as Thorndike had hypothesized, in 1898; see above).

According to Edelman, each time we adapt to an environmental challenge, neuronal groups are recalled from memory, then reentered after use. The more often their use results in our successfully meeting the challenge, the more likely we are to retrieve the same association and the more resistant to extinction it becomes; conversely, ineffective associations will become more likely to not survive.

In the chapters that follow, the reader will encounter a world of challenging learning and memory exercises. These are, perhaps, what Ramon y Cajal had in mind when he wrote of cerebral gymnastics, and we have seen evidence above of how such gymnastics might work. We imagine that the *Brainfit* program might lead to the formation of new and useful brain connections—perhaps initially in closed-loop circuits but eventually in reverberating cell assemblies and phase sequences—as initially conceived of by Hebb; unnecessary connections will be pruned, as described by Huttenlocher, Dawkins, and Young; the fittest connections, that is, those that are found to best serve the purpose of learning and memory, will survive, as theorized by Edelman. To all of this neural activity, the laws of association of Aristotle, Locke, Mill, and Ebbinghaus will still apply, as well as Thorndike's law of effect and Lashley's law of equipotentiality.

It is important to recognize that this plastic process will not only occur when the reader is immersed in the *Brainfit* program—it will be ongoing throughout the lifespan, whether we are consciously seeking to improve our learning and memory or simply passively experiencing the world about us. Neural plasticity, in one form or another, is an inescapable accompaniment of our existence. *Brainfit* seeks to channel this plasticity into new connections, the neural representations of mental strategies that will be maximally effective and efficient, making Neural Darwinism work to our benefit.

References

Aristotle. *De Memoria et Reminiscentia.* Cited in E. G. Boring (1957). *A History of Experimental Psychology* (2nd edition). New York: Appleton-Century-Crofts Publishing.

Cahill, L., & McGaugh, J. L. (1966). "Modulation of Memory Storage." *Current Opinion in Neurobiology, 6,* 237–242.

Chugani, H. T., Phelps, M. E., & Mazziotta, J. C. (1987). "Positron Emission Tomography Study of Human Brain Function Development." *Annals of Neurology, 22,* 487–97.

Dawkins, R. (1971). Selective neuron death as a possible memory mechanism. *Nature, 229,* 118–119.

Descartes, R. (1662). *Trait de L'homme.* Cited in E.G. Boring (1957). *A History of Experimental Psychology* (2nd edition). New York: Appleton-Century-Crofts Publishing.

Diamond, M. C., Krech, D., & Rozenzweig, M. (1964). The effects of enriched environment on the histology of the rat cerebral cortex. *Journal of Comparative Neurology, 123,* 111–119.

Diamond, M.C., Law, F., Rhodes, H., Lindner, B., Rozenzweig, M. R., Krech, D., & Bennett, E. L. (1966). "Increases in Cortical Depth and Glia Numbers in Rats Subjected to Enriched Environment." *Journal of Comparative Neurology, 128,* 117–125.

Ebbinghaus, H. (1985). *Ueber das Gedachtnis* Re-published in 1964 as *Memory: A Contribution to Experimental Psychology.* New York: Dover Publications.

Edelman, G. (1987). *Neural Darwinism.* New York: Basic Books.

Flourens, P. (1842). *Examen de la Phrenologie.* Cited in E.G. Boring (1957). *A history of experimental psychology* (2nd edition). New York: Appleton-Century-Crofts Publishing.

Glucksmann A. (1951). "Cell Death in Normal Vertebrate Ontogeny." *Biological Reviews, 26,* 59–86

Greenough, W. T., & Volkmar, F. R. (1973). "Pattern of Dendritic Branching in Occipital Cortex of Rats Reared in Complex Environments." *Experimental Neurology, 40,* 491–504.

Hebb, D. O. (1949). *The Organization of Behavior.* New York: John Wiley and Sons.

Hobbs, T. (1650). "Humaine Nature: Or the Fundamental Elements of Policie." Cited in J. C. A. Gaskin (Ed.), 1999, *Human Nature (Oxford World's Classics).* Oxford, UK: Oxford Paperbacks.

Huttenlocher, P. R. (1979). Synaptic Density in Human Frontal Cortex—Developmental Changes of Aging, *Brain Research, 163,* 195–205.

James, W. (1890). *Principles of Psychology.* London: Macmillan.

Jones, E. G. (1994). The neuron doctrine, *Journal of History of Neuroscience, 3,* 3-20.

Korsakoff, S. S. (1889). "Etude Medico-Psychologique Sur Un Forme Des Maladies De La Memoire." *Revue Philosophique, 5,* 501–530.

Lashley, K. S. (1950). "In Search of the Engram." *Society of Experimental Biology Symposium No. 4: Physiological Mechanisms in Animal Behavior.* New York: Cambridge University Press.

Locke, J. (1690). "Essay Concerning Human Understanding." Available in the public domain at: http://www.arts.cuhk.edu.hk/Philosophy/Locke/echu/.

Lynch, G. & Cotman, C. (1976). The hippocampus as a model for studying anatomical plasticity in the adult brain. In R Isaacson & K. Pribram (Eds.), *The Hippocampus.* (pp. 123–154). New York: Plenum Press.

Maril, A., Simons, J. S., Mitchell, J. P., Schwartz, B. L. & Schacter, D. L. (2003). "Feeling-of-Knowing in Episodic Memory: An Event-Related fMRI Study." *NeuroImage, 18,* 827–836.

McConnell, J. V. (1962). "Memory Transfer through Cannibalism in Planarians. *Journal of Neuropsychiatry, 3,* 42–48.

References

McGaugh, J. L. (1973). "Drug Facilitation of Learning and Memory." *Annual Review of Pharmacology, 13*, 229–241.

McGaugh, J. L. (1992[a]) "Hormones and Memory." *The Encyclopedia of Learning and Memory.* New York: Macmillan.

McGaugh, J. L. (1992[b]). "Memory Consolidation." *The Encyclopedia of Learning and Memory.* New York: Macmillan.

Mill, J. S. (1843). *The Logic of the Moral Sciences.* Re-issued in 1992 by Open Court.

Poldrack, R. A. & Gabrieli, J. D. E. (2001). Characterizing the neural mechanisms of skill learning and repetition priming. *Brain, 124*, 67–82.

Posner, M. E. & Raichle, M. (1994). *Images of Mind.* New York: W. H. Freeman.

Ramon y Cajal, S. (1904). "The Croonian Lecture: La Fine Structure des Centres Nerveux." *Proceedings of the Royal Society of London, 55*, 444–468.

Ramon y Cajal, S. (1909, 1911) *Histologie du Système Nerveux de L'homme et des Vertebras.* (translated by L. Azoulay). Paris: Maloine.

Rolando, L. (1809).*Saggio sopra la vera struttura del cerbello e sopra le funzioni del sistema nervosa.* Cited in Caputo, F., Spaziante, R., De Divitiis 7 Nashold, B.S. (1995). Luigi Rolando and his pioneering efforts to relate structure to function in the nervous system. *Journal of Neurosurgery, 83*, 933–937.

Rosenzweig, M., Krech, D., & Bennet, E. L. (1961). "Heredity, Environment, Brain Biochemistry, and Learning. *Current Trends in Psychological Theory.* Pittsburgh: University of Pittsburgh.

Rosenzweig, M., Krech, D., Bennett, e. L., & Diamond, M.C. (1962). "Effects of Environmental Complexity and Training on Brain Chemistry and Anatomy: A Replication and Extension. *Journal of Comparative and Physiological Psychology, 55*, 429–437.

Shepherd, G. M. (1991) *Foundations of the Neuron Doctrine.* New York: Oxford University Press.

Temple, E., Poldrack, R. A., Deutsch, G. K., Miller, S., Tallal, P., Merzinich, M. M., & Gabrieli, J. D. E. (2003). "Neural Deficits in Children with Dyslexia Ameliorated by Behavioral Remediation: Evidence from fMRI." *Proceeding of the National academy of Sciences, 100*, 2860–2865.

Thompson, R. (1957a). "The Comparative Effects of Shock and Anoxia on Memory." *Journal of Comparative and Physiological Psychology, 50*, 397–400.

Thompson, R. (1957b). "The Effect of ECS on Retention in Young and Adult Rats." *Journal of Comparative and Physiological Psychology, 50,* 644–646.

Thompson, R. (1958). "The Effects of Intracranial Stimulation on Memory in Cats." *Journal of Comparative and Physiological Psychology, 51*, 41–426.

Thompson, R., & McConnell, J. V. (1955). "Classical Conditioning in the Planarian, *Dugesia Dorotocephala.*" *Journal of Comparative and Physiological Psychology, 48*, 54–68.

Thompson, R., & Pennington, D. R. (1957). "Memory Decrement Produced by ECS as a Function of Distribution in Original Learning." *Journal of Comparative and Physiological Psychology, 50*, 4-1-404.

Thorndike, E. L. (1898). "Animal Intelligence: An Experimental Study of the Associative Process in Animals." *Psychological Monographs, No. 8.*

Thorndike (1905), *The Elements of Psychology.* New York: A. G. Seile.

Von Restorff, H. (1933). "Über die Wirkung von Bereichsbildungen im Spurenfeld." *Psychologische Forschungen, 18*, 199–342.

Wundt, W. (1873). *Grundzuge der Physiologischen Psychologie.* Cited in G. S. Hall (1912), *Founders of Modern Psychology.* New York: Appleton.

Young, J. Z. (1964). *A Model for the Brain.* Oxford, UK: Clarendon Press.

Young, J. Z. (1978). *Programs of the Brain.* Oxford, UK: Oxford University Press.

Notes

Chapter One

1. Will Block, "Galantamine Suppresses Brain-Cell Suicide," *Life Enhancement* magazine, February 2004, http://www.life-enhancement.com/LE/article_ template.asp?ID=912.

2. Dr. Gary Small. *The Memory Bible: An Innovative Strategy for Keeping Your Brain Young.* (New York: Hyperion, 2003), 2.

3. Monika Guttman, "The Aging Brain," *USC Health Magazine,* November 18, 2003, http://www.usc.edu/hsc/info/pr/hmm/01spring/brain.html.

4. Elizabeth Gould, "Study: Brain Regenerates Cells," *Newsweek* (Feb. 18, 2003): 12.

5. Kornack and Rakic, "Spotting New Brain Cells," *Newsweek* (Feb. 18, 2002): 00.

6. Dr. Richard Restak. *Mozart and the Fighter Pilot.* (New York: Three Rivers Press, 2002), 15.

7. http://www.preweb.com/releases/2002/9/prweb47048.htm

8. Fergus Craik, "Thanks for the Memories," *Newsweek,* Spring/Summer 2001: 55.

9. Small, *The Memory Bible,* 9.

10. You can find information about the Alzheimer's Foundation of America online at http://www.alzfdn.org/ or by calling 866-232-8484.

11. Dr. D. P Devenand. *The Memory Program.* (Hoboken: Wiley, 2001), 16–18.

12. Memory Assessment Clinic, Bethesda, Maryland. http://www.healthcentral.com/cooltools/ct_mental-health/ct_memory-quiz.cfm.

13. Some of the questions in the Brainy Knowledge Quiz come from World Wide Web sources including Education at Bristol (http://www.at-bristol.org.uk/Education/nesta/brain.htm), Brain Connection (http://www.brainconnection.com/library/?main=explorehome/brain-facts), and Enchanted Learning (http://www.enchantedlearning.com/subjects/anatomy/brain/Neuron.shtml).

Chapter Two

1. "Mild Cognitive Impairment," University of California at San Francisco Web site, http://memory.ucsf.edu/Education/education_mci.html.

2. Kathryn Wetzel, Ph.D. and Kathleen Harmeyer, MS. *Mind Games: The Aging Brain and How to Keep It Healthy.* (Albany: Delmar, 2000), 105–106. The table comes from this book and is used by permission.

3. Anne Underwood and Russell Watson, "Mind, Moods, and Stress: Thanks for the Memories." *Newsweek* Special Issue (Summer/Fall 2001), p. 56. Exercise concept from Sarah Reusing, Ph.D., John Hopkins University.

4. Ibid.

5. Adapted from the Neuro Gym, the University of Wales, Bangor: http://bangor.ac.uk/~mas009/neuro-gym/exercises/numbers.htm.

6. "Models of Human Memory," School of Psychology, Massey University, New Zealand: http://evolution.massey.ac.nz/assign2/AY/page1.html.

Chapter Three

1. Reprinted with permision of Scribner, an imprint of Simon & Schuster Adult Publishing Group, from THE OLD MAN AND THE SEA by Ernest Hemingway. Copyright 1952 by Ernest Hemingway. Copyright renewed (c) 1980 by Mary Hemingway.

2. T. S Eliot. "Preludes," Stanza One. First printed in *Blast* (July 1915). Reprinted by Donald Gallop, *T. S. Eliot: A Bibliography* (London: Faber and Faber, 1969): A1, C19. Poem originally published in Eliot's first book *Prufrock and Other Observations* (London: The Egoist, 1917): 24–26.

3. George A. Miller. "The Magical Number Seven Plus or Minus Two: Some Limits on Our Capacity for Processing Information, *Psychological Review* (63) pp. 81–97.

4. The study is reported in a CNN Interactive article found at the URL http://www.cnn.com/HEALTH/9808/19/stress.memory/

5. Randolph E. Schmid. Associated Press, "Stress Linked to Forgetfulness," *Boston Globe* (October 29, 2004) p. A-4.

Chapter Four

1. Allen D. Bragdon and David Gamon, Ph.D. *Use It or Lose It.*
Concept adapted from *Use It or Lose It: How to Protect Your Most Valuable Possession* by Allen Bragdon and David Gamon. (South Yarmouth: Allen D. Bragdon Publishers, Inc., 2000): 40–47.

Chapter Five

1. "Ginko Biloba," University of Maryland Web site, http://www.umm.edu/altmed/ConsHerbs/Ginkgo Bilobach.html.

Chapter Six

1. Dr. Philip Norrie, "The Magic-Ol Resveratol," *Alcohol in Moderation Digest* (Mar. 21, 2005): http//www.aim-digest.com/gateway/pages/general/articles/antiox/resver2.htm.

2. American Academy of Anti-Aging Medicine, "Red Wine Molecule May Protect Brain from Alzheimer's," http://www.worldhealth.net/p/230,4937.html. First reported by www.ruetershealth.com (Dec. 31, 2003).

Chapter Seven

1. Dr. David Snowdon. *Aging with Grace: What the Nun Study Teaches Us about Leading Longer, Healthier, and more Meaningful Lives.* (New York: Bantam, 2002) 177–180.

2. Donald R. Hall, DrPh, CHES, and Paula J. Wart, "B Vitamins Help Memory," HEALTHPlus Health and Wellness, Vanderbilt University, http://vanderbiltowc.wellsource.com/dh/Content.asp?ID=1625 (Aug. 3, 2004).

Chapter Eight

1. Sharon Begley. "Scans of Monks' Brains Show Meditation Alters Structure, Functioning," *Science Journal* (Nov. 5, 2004): http//:home.att.net/~meditation/monks.brains.html.

Chapter Nine

1. K. Warner Schaie. "Developmental Influences on Adult Intelligence: The Seattle Longitudinal Study." (Oxford: Oxford University Press): 0195156730, 1999.

2. Richard Restak, M.D. *Mozart's Brain and the Fighter Pilot.* (New York: Harmony Books, 2001): 88.

Chapter Ten

1. The Study Skills Help Page by Dr. Carolyn Hopper, Learning Strategies Coordinator for the Developmental Studies Department at Middle Tennessee State University. http://www.mtsu.edu/~studskl/hd/hemispheric_dominance.html.

2. Senior Health, http://seniorhealth.about.com/library/weekly/aa121801a.htm (summerizing from a University of Arizona study, published in *Psychological Science*, 2002.

3. "Caffeine Boosts Memory in Older Adults," Reuters Health, Prevent Disease.com, http://preventdisease.com/news/articles/caffeine_boosts_memory_in_adults.shtml.

4. "Putting Caffeine on Skin Lowers Risk of Cancer in Lab Mice," Health and Behavior, *USA Today*, http://www.usatoda.com/news/health/2002/08-26-caffeine_x.htm.

Chapter Eleven

1. http://www.lotsofjokes.com/cat_359.htm.

2. Christie Aschwanden, "A Walk a Day Keeps the Brain OK," SAGE News & Views, 3/22/04, http://www.sagecrossroads.net/Default.aspx?tabid=28&newsType=ArticleView&articleId.

3. "Stress and the Brain," http://www.brainconnections.com/topics/?main=fa/zebras.

4. Dr. Gene Cohen, M.D., Ph.D. *The Creative Age.* (New York: HarperCollins, 2000).